The Ancient Apothecary Book Revived

The Home Guide to Making and Using 150+ Potent Herbal Remedies for Natural Healing and Holistic Wellness (Including Preparation of Tinctures, Herbal Teas, Salves etc.)

(Herbal Recipes Series, Book 1)

By

Elena Silva

Disclaimer

This publication is designed to provide reliable information on the subject matter only for educational purposes, and it is not intended to provide medical advice for any medical treatment. You should always consult your doctor or physician for guidance before you stop, start, or alter any prescription medications or attempt to implement the methods discussed. This book is published independently by the author and has no affiliation with any brands or products mentioned within it. The author hereby disclaims any responsibility or liability whatsoever that is incurred from the use or application of the contents of this publication by the purchaser or reader. The purchaser or reader is hereby responsible for his or her own actions.

Other Books By Elena Silva

The Ancient Apothecary Book of Advanced Herbal Remedies (Herbal Recipes Series, Book 2)

Table of Contents

About The Author

Elena Silva is a seasoned herbalist, holistic wellness educator, and lifelong student of plant wisdom. With over two decades of experience rooted in both traditional and contemporary herbal practices, she has guided thousands toward natural healing through the art of home herbalism.

Elena's journey began in her grandmother's kitchen garden, where the scent of chamomile and mint first sparked a lifelong devotion to plants. Her deep respect for ancient healing traditions is paired with a modern, accessible teaching style that empowers everyday people to reclaim their health using simple, time-tested remedies.

Through workshops, community apothecary programs, and now this book series, she brings herbalism back to its roots: the home. When she's not tending herbs or writing, Elena leads workshops and teaches others how to bring herbal healing back into everyday life.

"I believe everyone has a healer within them—plants simply help us remember."
— Elena Silva

Introduction

What Is Home Apothecary?

Imagine stepping into your kitchen and, instead of reaching for a pharmaceutical bottle, your hand moves instinctively toward a jar of calendula petals, a dried root, or a bottle of golden-infused oil you made yourself. That's the beginning of **home apothecary**—a personal, sacred space where healing begins with plants, and wellness is built with intention, not just reaction.

Home apothecary is more than shelves of herbs and bottles; it is a living, evolving expression of self-care, family care, and connection with nature. It's your collection of thoughtfully chosen herbs, preparations, and tools that support your daily health naturally. Whether you're tending a sick child with chamomile tea or making your own salve for dry hands, this apothecary becomes your hands-on response to life's everyday ailments.

In ancient times, every village had its herbalist. Today, your home can reclaim that role. Your apothecary doesn't need to be large—it may start with just a few jars, a teapot, and a book like this. Over time, it becomes a trusted companion and a quiet reminder that healing doesn't have to come with side effects or insurance claims.

Why Choose Herbal Remedies?

We live in a world of incredible medical advancements, but we're also seeing a quiet return to the ancient knowledge of herbal medicine. Why? Because people are realizing that **health is more than the absence of illness—it's the presence of balance, energy, and connection.** Herbal remedies offer us something conventional medicine often can't: participation in our own wellness.

Herbs are not just about treating symptoms. They support the body's natural ability to heal itself. Ginger doesn't just ease nausea—it warms the body, stimulates digestion, and circulates life back into our system. Lavender isn't merely calming—it teaches the nervous system to soften, to breathe.

Many of us have grown weary of long ingredient lists and synthetic compounds. Herbs invite us to slow down, learn the story of each plant, and personalize our approach to healing. Herbal medicine helps us shift from being passive patients to empowered participants.

And perhaps most beautifully: herbalism encourages **respect**—for our bodies, for the plants, and for the earth that gives them.

Principles of Natural Healing & Holistic Wellness

This book isn't about "alternative" medicine. It's about remembering what was once the norm: that **healing is not a transaction—it's a relationship.**

Natural healing is rooted in the idea that the body is wise. Illness is often a signal, not just a malfunction. The body wants to return to balance, and plants have evolved for millennia to help us do just that.

Holistic wellness means we don't look at headaches as isolated from stress, or poor sleep as unrelated to digestion. We see the person as a whole: body, mind, spirit, and lifestyle. We also see plants as whole beings—not just sources of extracted chemicals, but allies with personality, energy, and intelligence.

The core principles you'll find throughout this book are:

- **Wholeness:** Treating the person, not just the condition
- **Prevention:** Supporting health proactively, not reactively
- **Personalization:** No two bodies—or remedies—are the same
- **Simplicity:** Healing doesn't have to be complex or expensive
- **Empowerment:** You are your family's first herbalist

This approach doesn't require perfection. It simply invites curiosity, consistency, and a deeper trust in the wisdom both your body and nature already carry.

How to Use This Book

You don't need to read this book front to back—though you certainly can. Think of it as a **practical guide, a reference manual, and a companion** to your herbal journey.

- If you're brand new to herbalism, start with the first few chapters. They'll introduce you to herbal actions, essential tools, and the mindset of a home healer.
- If you're ready to dive into recipes, skip to the preparation chapters. You'll find over **150+ carefully curated remedies**, arranged by form—teas, tinctures, balms—and by purpose: sleep, digestion, stress, skin, and more.
- If you want to address a specific issue—like menstrual cramps or seasonal allergies—head to the ailment-based chapters.
- For those who enjoy learning slowly and practically, try following the seasons. Use this book throughout the year to experiment with remedies that suit your needs as they change with the weather and your life.

Each recipe is designed to be beginner-friendly, with easy-to-source ingredients, clear steps, and dosage suggestions. You'll also find guidance on when to use certain herbs, how to store them, and how to make herbalism an intuitive part of your everyday routine.

We'll also help you make informed, responsible choices—because herbalism isn't just about "natural," it's about *intentional*.

Safety, Ethics, and Legal Disclaimer

This book is educational. It's not a substitute for medical advice, diagnosis, or treatment from a licensed practitioner. While herbs are powerful and generally safe when used properly, they are **not risk-free**, especially if used incorrectly or in combination with pharmaceuticals. Always consult a qualified healthcare provider before beginning any new regimen—especially during pregnancy, with children, or if you have a pre-existing condition.

That said, herbalism is also a powerful way to *reduce* dependency on unnecessary medications. The goal here is balance—**to integrate traditional knowledge responsibly in a modern world.**

Ethically, we also have a duty to respect the **sources** of our medicine. Many of the herbs we use come from Indigenous traditions and global communities. Use with gratitude and mindfulness. Harvest or purchase responsibly, and always ensure that your practices support sustainable ecosystems and fair labor.

Your role is not just to be a maker of remedies—but a steward of wisdom.

Final Words Before We Begin…

If you've ever wanted to feel more confident in caring for your body… if you've longed to break up with over-the-counter drugs… if you've wanted to return to something more **earth-centered, soul-aligned, and truly nourishing**—you're in the right place.

Let this book be your doorway into a world that is **ancient but never outdated, natural but never naive**, and **personal but never isolating.**

You are not just learning about herbs.
You are remembering something your ancestors already knew.

Let's begin.

Part I: The Foundations of Herbalism

Chapter 1

A Brief History of Herbal Medicine

Herbal Traditions Across Cultures

Herbal medicine is one of the oldest systems of healing known to humankind. Long before microscopes or pharmacies, people everywhere turned to the plants around them for food, comfort, and medicine. And remarkably, different cultures on different continents—despite never meeting—often discovered the same plants and healing techniques.

In **India**, the healing system known as **Ayurveda** has thrived for over 3,000 years. Here, herbs like **turmeric, tulsi (holy basil)**, and **ashwagandha** are used to balance energy, calm the mind, and support digestion. In **Traditional Chinese Medicine (TCM)**, practitioners use herbs like **ginseng, licorice root**, and **schisandra** to strengthen life force—called *Qi*—and restore harmony in the body.

In **Africa**, herbalists—often called bush doctors or traditional healers—have long used plants such as **baobab, aloe**, and **kinkeliba** to treat wounds, infections, and fevers. Meanwhile, **Native American tribes** in North America developed powerful plant-based systems using herbs like **yarrow, echinacea**, and **black cohosh** for respiratory issues, pain, and women's health.

Across Europe, generations of women (often midwives and healers) used herbs in what we now call "folk medicine." Simple remedies—like nettle soup for anemia, elderflower tea for colds, or lavender satchels for sleep—were household staples. These traditions were passed orally, woman to woman, grandmother to granddaughter.

These global traditions may look different on the surface, but they're all built on a **deep respect for plants**, seasonal rhythms, and natural balance. And although times have changed, the wisdom endures.

The Evolution of Home Remedies

As towns and cities grew and medical science advanced, herbalism didn't disappear—it simply adapted. In earlier centuries, most households in Europe and America had a "still room" or herbal corner. This was where herbs were dried, ointments made, and syrups bottled.

Even doctors in the 1800s and early 1900s used plant-based remedies as their primary tools. For instance:

- **Willow bark** was used to reduce pain and inflammation (this led to the discovery of aspirin).
- **Foxglove** (digitalis) was used for heart conditions.
- **Chamomile**, still used today, was recommended for colicky infants and anxiety.

But with industrialization came the mass production of synthetic drugs. The medical system became more professionalized—and in some cases, **less personal**. Many herbal traditions were pushed aside as "old-fashioned," especially in the West.

Still, herbal knowledge never truly vanished. It lived on in rural areas, Indigenous communities, immigrant homes, and folk traditions.

Modern Resurgence of Herbal Healing

Today, herbalism is undergoing a powerful and exciting revival. More people are seeking natural alternatives to address issues like anxiety, fatigue, skin conditions, and immune support—without always relying on prescription drugs.

Why this return?

- **Mistrust of overmedication**: Many people feel overwhelmed by side effects, interactions, and the high costs of pharmaceuticals.
- **Desire for natural living**: The movement toward organic foods, clean skincare, and sustainable living has made herbalism a perfect fit.
- **Empowerment**: Learning about herbs gives people the ability to care for themselves and their families in a more connected, gentle way.

Best of all? You don't need to be a botanist or chemist. A basic understanding of herbs and a willingness to observe your body and environment is all you need to begin.

Chapter 2

Understanding Herbs and How They Work

Herbs don't heal you. They remind your body how to heal itself."

This chapter is where herbalism truly begins to feel alive. To use herbs effectively, you must first understand their nature—how they interact with the body, what their internal chemistry does, and how their personalities influence different people in different ways.

Let's break it down in a way that is **practical, intuitive, and empowering**—so that even if you're brand new, you'll walk away with a working knowledge of how plants support health.

Medicinal Properties of Herbs

Every plant contains a variety of **active constituents**—these are the natural chemicals that give the plant its healing abilities. Think of them as the "medicine molecules" inside each herb, formed by nature over thousands of years.

Here are a few **key medicinal properties**:

Herbal Property	What It Does	Examples
Anti-inflammatory	Reduces pain, swelling, irritation	Turmeric, calendula, willow bark
Antimicrobial	Fights bacteria, viruses, fungi	Garlic, thyme, oregano
Carminative	Relieves gas and bloating	Fennel, ginger, peppermint
Diuretic	Increases urination to flush toxins	Dandelion leaf, parsley
Demulcent	Soothes mucous membranes	Marshmallow root, slippery elm
Astringent	Tightens tissues, stops bleeding	Raspberry leaf, yarrow
Nervine	Calms or nourishes the nervous system	Chamomile, skullcap, lemon balm

Each herb may have **multiple properties**, and their effectiveness depends on **how they're prepared** (tea, tincture, salve, etc.), the part used (root, leaf, flower), and how they're stored.

Think of herbs as multidimensional—they don't just "do one thing." They work in the body **holistically**, often supporting several systems at once.

Herbal Actions: The Vocabulary of Healing Plants

Herbalists use specific terms to describe **how an herb behaves in the body**. These are called **herbal actions**. Learning this "language" is key to making your own formulas and choosing the right herbs for the job.

Here's a breakdown of essential actions:

Adaptogen

- Helps your body **adapt to stress** and restore balance in the nervous and hormonal systems.
- Great for: Burnout, chronic fatigue, hormonal imbalance
- Examples: Ashwagandha, holy basil (tulsi), rhodiola, eleuthero

Nervine

- Calms, nourishes, or stimulates the **nervous system**, depending on the herb.
- Great for: Anxiety, tension, sleeplessness, nervous exhaustion
- Examples: Chamomile, lemon balm, passionflower, skullcap

Tonic

- Strengthens and restores a particular **body system** over time with regular use.
- Great for: Weak digestion, depleted energy, fragile immunity
- Examples: Nettle (nutritive tonic), hawthorn (heart tonic), oatstraw (nervous system tonic)

Alterative (aka blood purifier)

- Gently stimulates the body's natural detox functions—especially the **liver, lymph, and skin**.
- Great for: Skin issues, sluggish digestion, chronic inflammation
- Examples: Burdock, cleavers, red clover

Expectorant

- Helps the lungs **clear mucus** by loosening or drying it up.
- Great for: Wet cough, congestion, bronchitis
- Examples: Mullein, elecampane, thyme

Emmenagogue

- Stimulates and regulates **menstrual flow**.
- Great for: Menstrual cramps, irregular periods (use with care in pregnancy)
- Examples: Ginger, yarrow, dong quai

💡 **Tip**: When selecting herbs, combine actions thoughtfully. For example, a blend for stress might include:

- An **adaptogen** (ashwagandha),
- A **nervine** (lemon balm), and
- A **tonic** (oatstraw) for long-term support.

How Herbs Interact With the Body

Unlike pharmaceutical drugs, which often target a **single receptor** or chemical in the body, herbs work **system-wide**, supporting the **natural intelligence** of your organs and tissues.

Herbs as Allies, Not Bosses

- A drug might **force** your body to do something (like induce sleep).
- An herb might **encourage** your body to regulate itself (like helping your body shift into rest mode).

Example:

- A pharmaceutical sedative might knock you out.
- Passionflower gently calms the nervous system so your body *chooses* rest.

Herbs Work Best When:

- Used at the **first sign** of an issue (e.g., echinacea at the first tickle in the throat)
- Taken **consistently over time** (like nettle for energy and minerals)
- Paired with **lifestyle support** (rest, hydration, nourishment)

Whole Plant Synergy

Each herb contains not just one active chemical, but **hundreds** of compounds that work **in harmony**. This makes herbs:

- Gentler
- Safer over time
- Less likely to cause harsh side effects

Herbal Energetics: Warm, Cool, Dry, Damp

One of the most ancient (and still relevant) ways to understand herbs is through **energetics**. Instead of just asking "What does this herb do?", we also ask "What kind of condition is it best for?"

Energetics describe:

- How a person **feels** (cold hands, dry throat, oily skin, sluggish digestion)
- How a plant **behaves** in the body (warms, moistens, cools, dries)

Warming Herbs

- Stimulate circulation, help with coldness, fatigue, slow digestion
- Examples: Ginger, cinnamon, cayenne, rosemary

Cooling Herbs

- Reduce heat, inflammation, irritation
- Examples: Peppermint, lemon balm, hibiscus, violet

Moistening Herbs

- Help dry skin, dry cough, constipation, or dehydration
- Examples: Marshmallow root, licorice, flaxseed

Drying Herbs

- Help damp conditions—think sinus congestion, sluggish digestion, or excess mucus
- Examples: Sage, yarrow, black tea, thyme

Real-Life Application:

Let's say you have a sore throat:

- If it's dry, scratchy, and irritated → choose a **moistening** herb like **marshmallow**.
- If it's hot, red, and inflamed → choose a **cooling** herb like **hibiscus**.
- If it's wet and mucusy → choose a **drying** herb like **sage**.
- If you're chilled and tired with it → choose a **warming** herb like **ginger**.

By learning to match herbs to **patterns** rather than just symptoms, you'll get better results and fewer side effects.

Chapter 3

Getting to Know Your Herbal Allies

"The first step in learning herbal medicine isn't memorizing remedies—it's forming relationships."

Before tinctures are made or teas are brewed, there must be **trust**—a quiet bond between the herbalist and the plant. In this chapter, we move from understanding how herbs work in the body (covered in Chapter 2) to discovering **who** these plants are, **how to meet them**, and **how to welcome them into your life**.

Getting to know your herbal allies means more than just identifying them by name. It's about observing how they grow, learning what they like, noticing how they smell and feel, and discovering how they affect different people. Some herbs will become like old friends you turn to again and again. Others might surprise you, revealing hidden powers or showing up when you least expect it.

In many traditional cultures, this relationship is sacred. Plants aren't just ingredients—they're **living beings** with their own rhythms, preferences, and temperaments. As you deepen your connection to them, you may start to feel this too.

In this chapter, you'll learn:

- How to recognize and categorize herbs by **plant family**
- How to **identify them in the wild or your garden**
- How to **source herbs** ethically and safely
- And how to begin **growing your own apothecary** right at home

By the end of this chapter, you won't just know *about* herbs—you'll have started to build your own circle of **green allies**, a network of living support for your body, your home, and your spirit.

Let's meet them.

Key Herbal Families

Understanding which family a plant belongs to is one of the fastest ways to begin seeing patterns in the herbal world. Just like humans have relatives that resemble each other in traits or personalities, herbs in the same botanical family often share similar actions, chemistry, appearance, or uses.

This knowledge helps you:

- Recognize plants faster in the wild or garden

- Predict the properties of a new plant

- Avoid allergic reactions (if you're sensitive to one member of a family, others may affect you similarly)

KEY HERBAL FAMILIES

MINT FAMILY
(LAMIACEAE)

Peppermint   Lemon balm

DAISY FAMILY
(ASTERACEAE)

Chamomile   Echinacea

CARROT FAMILY
(APIACEAE)

Fennel   Dill   Coriander

Fennel   Di   Coriander

MALLOW FAMILY
(MALVACEAE)

Hibiscus   Hollyhock

Marshmallow   Hollyhock

Let's take a closer look at some of the most important and beginner-friendly herbal families.

1. Lamiaceae – The Mint Family

This family includes many of the most beloved herbs in herbalism and the kitchen.

Common Members:

- Peppermint (*Mentha piperita*)

- Lemon Balm (*Melissa officinalis*)

- Lavender (*Lavandula angustifolia*)

- Rosemary (*Rosmarinus officinalis*)
- Sage (*Salvia officinalis*)
- Oregano (*Origanum vulgare*)
- Thyme (*Thymus vulgaris*)

Common Traits:

- Aromatic (strong scents from essential oils)
- Square stems
- Opposite leaves (leaves grow in pairs)
- Generally warming or cooling depending on preparation

Herbal Uses:

- **Digestive support** (peppermint, thyme)
- **Calming the nervous system** (lemon balm, lavender)
- **Respiratory health** (sage, thyme)
- **Antibacterial and antifungal** (oregano, rosemary)

Why they're beginner-friendly: Mints are easy to grow, pleasant to taste, and extremely versatile. Many can be used both medicinally and culinarily.

2. Asteraceae – The Daisy Family

This is one of the largest plant families in the world, and many of its members are healing powerhouses.

Common Members:

- Chamomile (*Matricaria recutita*)
- Echinacea (*Echinacea purpurea*)
- Calendula (*Calendula officinalis*)
- Yarrow (*Achillea millefolium*)
- Dandelion (*Taraxacum officinale*)

Common Traits:

- Flower heads made up of a central disk and ray petals

- Often yellow, white, or purple flowers

- May cause allergic reactions in sensitive individuals

Herbal Uses:

- **Immune support** (echinacea)

- **Skin healing & wound care** (calendula, yarrow)

- **Anti-inflammatory** (chamomile, calendula)

- **Liver and digestive support** (dandelion)

Note: Chamomile tea is incredibly gentle and well-tolerated, making it a perfect first herbal ally.

3. Apiaceae – The Carrot Family

This family contains many culinary spices and medicinal herbs, but also includes some poisonous plants—so **accurate identification is essential**.

Common Members:

- Fennel (*Foeniculum vulgare*)

- Dill (*Anethum graveolens*)

- Coriander/Cilantro (*Coriandrum sativum*)

- Angelica (*Angelica archangelica*)

- Lovage (*Levisticum officinale*)

Common Traits:

- Feathery, lace-like leaves

- Umbrella-shaped flower clusters (*umbels*)

- Aromatic seeds and roots

Herbal Uses:

- **Digestive support and gas relief** (fennel, dill)

- **Lung and expectorant support** (angelica)

- **Hormonal and reproductive support** (some angelicas)

⚠ Caution: This family also includes **poison hemlock**. Never wild-harvest Apiaceae plants unless you are *absolutely* sure of your ID.

4. Malvaceae – The Mallow Family

Known for its softening, soothing properties, this family features herbs that are incredibly gentle and moistening to tissues.

Common Members:

- Marshmallow (*Althaea officinalis*)

- Hibiscus (*Hibiscus sabdariffa*)

- Hollyhock (*Alcea rosea*)

- Okra (*Abelmoschus esculentus*)

Common Traits:

- Mucilaginous (slippery and soothing)

- Big, showy flowers

- Soft, broad leaves

Herbal Uses:

- **Soothing sore throats** (marshmallow)

- **Digestive tract support** (all mallow species)

- **Urinary tract soothing** (marshmallow root, hibiscus)

- **Cooling, astringent teas** (hibiscus)

These are perfect herbs for people with dry, irritated conditions. Their texture helps lubricate and heal from within.

How to Identify, Source, and Grow Herbs

Whether you're foraging wild nettle, buying dried chamomile from a herbal shop, or planting lemon balm in your garden, the process of identifying, sourcing, and growing herbs is one of the most rewarding parts of being a home herbalist. It builds confidence, cultivates awareness, and creates a lasting connection to the plants you work with.

Identifying Herbs: The Herbalist's Eye

Learning to recognize herbs in the wild—or even in your backyard—is a foundational skill in herbalism. It takes time, attention, and practice, but it's deeply satisfying.

Basic Steps to Identify an Herb:

1. **Observe the Shape and Arrangement of Leaves**
   - Are the leaves smooth or serrated?
   - Are they opposite (paired), alternate, or whorled around the stem?
   - What shape are they—oval, lance-shaped, heart-like?

2. **Examine the Flower and Stem**
   - Flowers are key! Count the petals and look at their arrangement.
   - What's the color, scent, size, and texture?
   - Does the stem have ridges? Is it hairy or smooth?

3. **Use Your Senses**
   - **Smell** the crushed leaf—minty, earthy, spicy, floral?
   - **Touch** the texture of the leaves—is it soft, rough, sticky, or fuzzy?
   - Be cautious with taste unless you're 100% sure it's edible and safe.

4. **Study the Growing Environment**
   - Does it grow in shade or sun?
   - Near water or in dry soil?
   - Alone or in clusters?

Tools for Identification:

- A trusted **field guide** for your region (with color photos)
- **Plant ID apps** like PlantNet or Seek (good as a secondary confirmation)
- A **hand lens** for closely inspecting leaves and flower structures
- **Notebooks** for drawing, pressing, or documenting findings

Tip: Never rely on one photo online to identify a plant. Many toxic plants mimic edible ones. Always cross-reference at least 2–3 trusted sources.

Sourcing Herbs: Where to Buy and What to Look For

When purchasing herbs—especially when starting out—it's essential to focus on **purity, quality, and ethical sourcing**.

Types of Herbs You Can Buy:

- **Dried whole herbs or cut/sifted herbs** (leaves, flowers, bark, roots)
- **Powdered herbs** (good for capsules, not ideal for tea)
- **Tinctures and extracts** (liquid form)
- **Essential oils** (use with caution, very concentrated)

Best Places to Source Herbs:

- **Local herb shops or apothecaries** (if available)
- **Reputable online herbal companies**, such as:
  - Mountain Rose Herbs
  - Starwest Botanicals
  - Frontier Co-op
  - Indigo Herbs (UK)

Always check:

- **Origin**: Where was the herb grown?
- **Processing method**: Was it wildcrafted or cultivated?
- **Harvest date**: Freshness is key—aim for herbs harvested within the last 12–18 months
- **Certifications**: Organic, sustainably wildcrafted, non-GMO

What Quality Herbs Should Look Like:

- **Color**: Should be vibrant (not faded or greyish)
- **Aroma**: Should smell fragrant and distinct, not musty or stale
- **Texture**: Should still feel somewhat alive—not brittle, dusty, or crumbly

⚠ **Avoid bulk herbs from unknown sellers**, especially in marketplaces where storage and handling are unclear.

Growing Herbs: Bringing the Garden to Your Apothecary

Growing herbs yourself is empowering. Even with limited space, anyone can cultivate a few key medicinal plants. You control the quality, harvest fresh material, and deepen your relationship with the plants you use.

Where to Grow:

- **Balconies** and windowsills (containers or pots)
- **Raised beds** or **garden plots**
- **Vertical gardens** or hanging baskets for small spaces

What Herbs Need:

- **Sunlight** – Most medicinal herbs like 4–8 hours/day of full sun
- **Soil** – Well-draining, neutral to slightly alkaline is ideal
- **Water** – Varies by plant, but most need consistent moisture without sogginess
- **Spacing** – Avoid overcrowding to prevent fungal growth and root competition

Easy Beginner Herbs to Grow:

Herb	Benefits	Growing Tips
Chamomile	Calming, sleep, digestion	Grows well in full sun; reseeds easily
Peppermint	Digestion, headaches	Loves moisture, spreads rapidly—best in pots
Calendula	Skin, inflammation	Thrives in sun; pick flowers often to encourage more
Basil (Tulsi)	Anti-stress, immune support	Keep in warm weather, pinch back flowers
Lemon Balm	Anxiety, insomnia	Grows in partial shade, slightly invasive
Thyme	Respiratory health	Prefers dry soil, compact and hardy

Harvesting & Drying

- Harvest **in the morning** after dew dries, before full sun
- For **leaves**, snip just above a leaf node to encourage regrowth
- For **flowers**, pick when freshly opened
- For **roots**, harvest in the fall when the plant stores energy

Dry herbs **in bundles** (upside-down), on screens, or in paper bags. Store in **airtight glass jars**, labeled with the name and date.

HERB DRYING GUIDE

HARVEST FRESH HERBS

TIE IN SMALL BUNDLES

HANG TO DRY

STORE IN

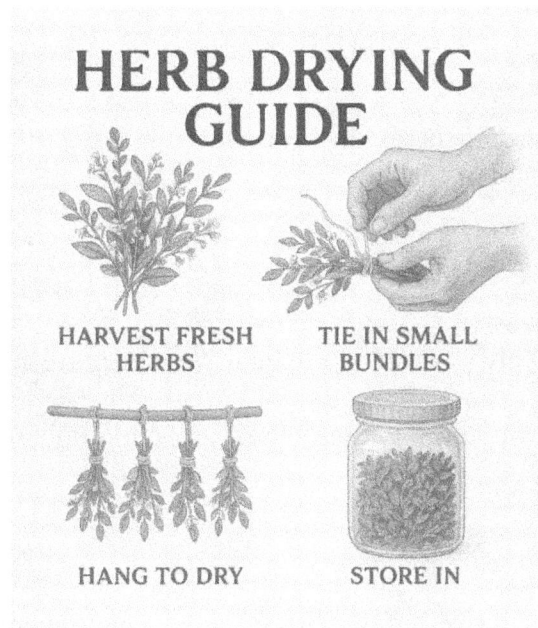

Storage Tip: Keep your jars in a cool, dark place. Sunlight breaks down herbal potency over time.

Bonus: Why Growing Your Own Herbs Changes Everything

- You'll begin to *observe the plants more deeply*—not just what they do, but how they grow, smell, react, and communicate.
- You'll know exactly what's in your remedy—no pesticides, no fillers, just pure plant energy.
- It brings a **ritual of healing** into your daily life. Even watering a calendula plant becomes an act of wellness.

Organic vs. Wildcrafted vs. Cultivated

As you begin building your apothecary, you'll come across different types of herbs based on **how they were grown or harvested**. Understanding the differences can help you make ethical, potent, and sustainable choices.

Organic Herbs

What it means: These herbs are grown on farms that follow strict organic standards—no synthetic fertilizers, pesticides, or GMOs.

Pros:

- Safer for internal use
- Better for the environment and farmworkers
- Usually certified and traceable

Things to Watch:

- May be more expensive
- "Organic" doesn't always mean high quality—check freshness, color, and scent

Best for: Daily use, teas, tinctures, culinary uses, and children's remedies

Wildcrafted Herbs

What it means: These are harvested directly from their natural environment—forests, mountains, meadows—without cultivation. True wildcrafting is done with **respect, knowledge, and restraint**

Pros:

- Often more potent and energetically vibrant
- Reflects the plant's natural habitat and power

Risks:

- Can be overharvested and ecologically damaging
- Quality varies greatly based on who harvested it
- Some wild areas may be contaminated (e.g., near roads, polluted soil)

Ethical Wildcrafting Rule:

"Take only what you need, never more than one-third, and only if the population is healthy and abundant."

Best for: Energetic medicine, spiritual work, or when you have knowledge of the source

Cultivated Herbs

What it means: These are herbs grown in controlled settings—either by you in your garden or by farmers (organic or non-organic). Cultivated doesn't necessarily mean organic unless specified.

Pros:

- Easy to grow at home
- Consistent quality
- Affordable and accessible

Risks:

- Lower potency in some species if not grown in ideal soil/sun conditions
- Commercial farm herbs may be sprayed or irradiated if not certified

Best for: Homemade remedies, teas, and garden apothecaries

Quick Comparison Table

Type	Source	Best For	Watch Out For
Organic	Certified organic farms	Safe daily use, internal remedies	Higher cost, freshness may vary
Wildcrafted	Wild-harvested (ethical)	Deep healing, ritual use	Overharvesting, lack of traceability
Cultivated	Garden/farm grown (non-certified)	Easy home apothecaries	Pesticide use if not organic

💡 Final Thought

There's no "best" option overall—it depends on your **needs**, your **values**, and your **access**. For example:

- Want control? → **Grow your own.**
- Want convenience and purity? → **Buy organic.**
- Want potent and wild? → **Ethical wildcrafting.**

Whether you're foraging in a field, shopping online, or watching a seed sprout in your windowsill, you are becoming an **active participant** in your own medicine-making. The more you connect with the plant from root to remedy, the more powerful your herbal journey becomes.

But always—**respect the plant, the land, and the process.**

Part II: Building Your Home Apothecary

Chapter 4

Essential Tools and Ingredients

Creating herbal remedies at home doesn't require a high-tech laboratory. Most of the tools you'll need are already in your kitchen—or can be found easily online or at a local natural health store. Your tools don't have to be fancy—what matters is that they're clean, safe, and easy to use.

Equipment for Herbal Preparation

- **Mason jars or recycled glass jars** – Ideal for tinctures, infusions, oil extractions, and vinegars.
- **Measuring cups and spoons** – For accurate dosing and consistent recipes.
- **Strainers, cheesecloth, or muslin bags** – Used to separate herbs from liquids after infusion or extraction.
- **Funnels** – Helpful for transferring liquids into bottles and jars without mess.
- **Mortar and pestle or herb grinder** – For grinding dried herbs into powders or breaking up roots and seeds.
- **Double boiler or slow cooker** – For gently warming oils and butters when making salves and infused oils.
- **Digital kitchen scale (optional)** – For precise recipes, especially in larger batches.

Storage Materials

- **Amber or cobalt tincture bottles** – These protect herbal extracts from light, preserving potency.
- **Glass jars with airtight lids** – Use for storing bulk herbs or teas.
- **Dropper bottles** – Perfect for custom blends and easy application.
- **Metal tins or salve containers** – Use for creams, balms, and herbal rubs.

Base Ingredients

- **Carrier oils**: Extra virgin olive, sweet almond, grapeseed, or jojoba oil are common for infusions and skincare.
- **Alcohols**: Vodka (at least 80 proof) or brandy for tincture-making.
- **Apple cider vinegar**: A non-alcoholic alternative with its own healing properties.

- **Natural butters**: Shea butter, cocoa butter for body butters and salves.
- **Clays**: Kaolin, bentonite, and French green clay for facial masks, poultices, or detoxing baths.

✍ **Note**: Cleanliness is essential in herbal preparation. Wash and sterilize all tools before each use to prevent contamination or spoilage.

Chapter 5

Stocking Your Herbal Pantry

Your herbal pantry is like the spice rack of a healing kitchen—it's your go-to collection of herbs for teas, tinctures, compresses, and culinary medicine. With a thoughtfully stocked pantry, you can make hundreds of home remedies in minutes.

Top 40 Must-Have Herbs

(You don't need them all at once! Start with 5–10 and build from there.)

Chamomile (Matricaria chamomilla / Chamaemelum nobile)

Botanical Overview

- **Family:** Asteraceae (Daisy family)
- **Common Names:** German chamomile (M. chamomilla), Roman chamomile (C. nobile)
- **Parts Used:** Flowers
- **Plant Type:** Annual (German) or perennial (Roman)
- **Height:** 6–24 inches

Botanical Features

- **Flowers:** Small, daisy-like, with white petals and a yellow cone-shaped center

- **Leaves:** Finely divided, feathery, and aromatic
- **Aroma:** Sweet, apple-like scent

Growing & Harvesting

- **Conditions:** Full sun, well-drained soil
- **Harvest:** Pick flower heads when fully open; dry in shade for teas or salves

Medicinal Actions

- Calming nervine, digestive aid, anti-inflammatory
- Used for insomnia, gas, bloating, stress, and teething

⚠ Caution

- People with **ragweed allergies** may react to chamomile
- Always use organically grown chamomile to avoid contamination

Peppermint (Mentha × piperita)

Botanical Overview

- **Family:** Lamiaceae (Mint family)
- **Parts Used:** Leaves
- **Plant Type:** Perennial, spreads by runners
- **Height:** 1–3 feet

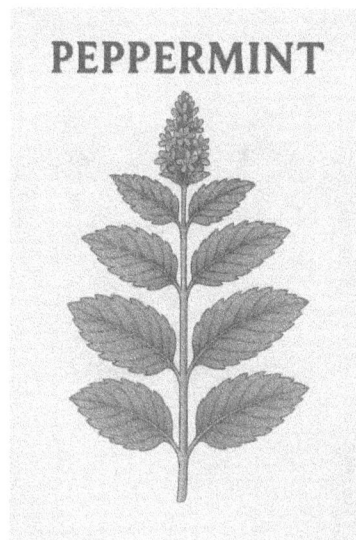

PEPPERMINT

Botanical Features

- **Leaves:** Dark green, serrated, and strongly aromatic
- **Stem:** Square-shaped (common to mint family)
- **Flowers:** Small, pale purple/lavender in whorls

Growing & Harvesting

- Thrives in moist soil, partial sun
- Best harvested in early morning before flowering for highest essential oil content

Medicinal Actions

- Antispasmodic, carminative, cooling
- Relieves indigestion, nausea, tension headaches, and muscle pain

⚠ Caution

- Not for infants or young children near the nose (risk of breathing difficulty)
- Avoid high doses in reflux sufferers (can relax esophageal sphincter)

Ginger (Zingiber officinale)

Botanical Overview

- **Family:** Zingiberaceae
- **Parts Used:** Rhizome (underground stem)
- **Plant Type:** Tropical perennial
- **Height:** 2–4 feet

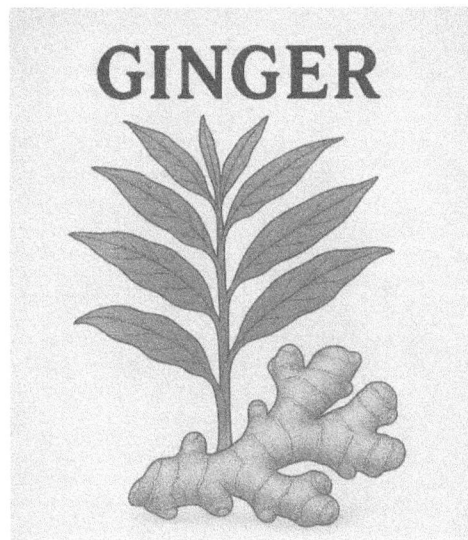

Botanical Features

- **Leaves:** Long, lance-shaped green leaves
- **Flowers:** Rare in temperate climates; pale yellow with purple tips
- **Rhizome:** Knobby, golden-yellow inside, aromatic and spicy

Growing & Harvesting

- Grows well in containers indoors or outside in warm climates
- Harvest once plant is mature (8–10 months); wash and dry rhizome

Medicinal Actions

- Warming, digestive, anti-inflammatory
- Used for motion sickness, nausea, circulation, and joint pain

⚠ Caution

- Can thin the blood—avoid before surgery
- Use with care in ulcers or gallstones

Lemon Balm (Melissa officinalis)

Botanical Overview

- **Family:** Lamiaceae (Mint family)
- **Parts Used:** Leaves
- **Plant Type:** Perennial herb
- **Height:** 1–2 feet

LEMON BALM

Botanical Features

- **Leaves:** Heart-shaped, serrated, lemon-scented
- **Flowers:** Tiny white or pale yellow, not very showy
- **Aroma:** Strong lemony fragrance when crushed

Growing & Harvesting

- Grows well in containers or garden beds; partial shade is ideal
- Harvest leaves before flowering for best potency

Medicinal Actions

- Nervine, carminative, antiviral
- Supports mood, digestion, and cold sore outbreaks

⚠ Caution

- May interfere with thyroid medications—consult your doctor if on thyroid treatment

Echinacea (Echinacea purpurea / angustifolia / pallida)

Botanical Overview

- **Family:** Asteraceae
- **Parts Used:** Root, flower, and leaves (depending on species)
- **Plant Type:** Perennial wildflower
- **Height:** 2–4 feet

ECHINACEA

Botanical Features

- **Flowers:** Cone-shaped pink-purple petals with a spiky orange-brown center
- **Leaves:** Long and lance-like with a slightly rough texture
- **Roots:** Used more in traditional applications (especially E. angustifolia)

Growing & Harvesting

- Prefers full sun and sandy, well-drained soil
- Roots harvested in 2nd or 3rd year of growth; flowers can be used fresh or dried

Medicinal Actions

- Immunomodulatory, anti-inflammatory, antimicrobial
- Used to shorten cold duration, reduce infections, and stimulate immune activity

⚠ Caution

- Best taken at onset of illness, not long-term
- May cause allergic reaction in people sensitive to daisy-family plants

Calendula (Calendula officinalis)

Botanical Overview

- **Family:** Asteraceae (Daisy family)
- **Common Names:** Pot marigold
- **Parts Used:** Flowers (petals and whole heads)
- **Plant Type:** Annual
- **Height:** 1–2 feet

CALENDULA

Botanical Features

- **Flowers:** Bright yellow to deep orange; daisy-like
- **Leaves:** Slightly sticky, oblong, and aromatic
- **Scent:** Mildly resinous, somewhat peppery

Growing & Harvesting

- Prefers full sun and well-drained soil
- Harvest when flowers are fully open; dry quickly in shade to preserve resins

Medicinal Actions

- Anti-inflammatory, vulnerary (wound healing), lymphatic
- Used in skin salves, wound washes, teas, and mouth rinses

⚠ Caution

- Rare skin sensitivity in some individuals when applied topically

Elderberry (Sambucus nigra)

Botanical Overview

- **Family:** Adoxaceae
- **Common Names:** Elder, Black Elder, European Elderberry
- **Parts Used:** Berries (ripe), Flowers
- **Plant Type:** Deciduous shrub or small tree
- **Height:** 5–12 feet (1.5–3.5 meters)
- **Native To:** Europe, North America, parts of Asia

ELDERBERRY

Botanical Characteristics

- **Leaves:** Opposite, compound leaves with 5–9 serrated leaflets, slightly rough to touch.
- **Flowers:** Creamy-white, flat-topped clusters (called umbels), blooming in early summer.
- **Berries:** Small, deep purple to black when ripe; form in heavy drooping clusters in late summer or early fall.
- **Stem/Bark:** Woody, pale brown, and dotted with lenticels (pores).

Growing & Harvesting

- **Growing Conditions:** Prefers moist, well-drained soil and full sun to part shade. Grows well near creeks or in gardens.
- **Propagation:** Easily propagated by cuttings or seeds.
- **Harvesting:**
    - **Flowers**: Collected in early summer just as buds open, dried for teas or syrups.
    - **Berries**: Only harvest **ripe**, dark purple berries—unripe ones are toxic when raw.

Medicinal Actions

- **Immune Modulator** – Stimulates immune response and shortens cold/flu duration.
- **Antiviral** – Especially against influenza viruses (contains flavonoids and anthocyanins).
- **Diaphoretic** – Helps induce gentle sweating during fever.
- **Antioxidant** – High in vitamin C and anthocyanins that protect cells.

⚠ Caution

- **Raw, unripe berries, bark, and leaves** contain **cyanogenic glycosides**, which can cause nausea, vomiting, or more serious toxicity. Always cook or dry berries before use.
- Do **not use if pregnant or nursing** without professional guidance.
- Elderflowers are generally safer and gentler than berries.

Fun Fact:

In European folklore, the elder tree was considered sacred and guarded by the "Elder Mother" spirit. Cutting it down without permission was thought to bring misfortune!

Nettle (Urtica dioica)

Botanical Overview

- **Family:** Urticaceae
- **Parts Used:** Leaves, seeds, roots
- **Plant Type:** Perennial
- **Height:** 2–6 feet

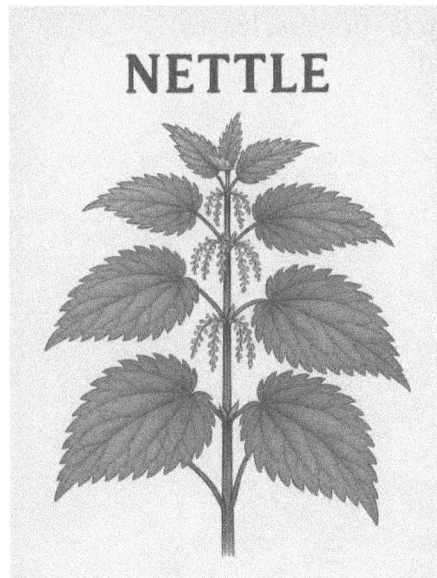

NETTLE

Botanical Features

- **Leaves:** Deep green, serrated, covered in tiny stinging hairs
- **Stem:** Square, bristled, often hollow
- **Flowers:** Tiny, greenish and not showy

Growing & Harvesting

- Prefers moist, rich soils; grows wild near rivers and ditches
- Wear gloves when harvesting young top leaves in spring

Medicinal Actions

- Nutritive tonic, anti-inflammatory, antihistamine
- Supports joint health, seasonal allergies, and nutrient replenishment

⚠ Caution

- Raw leaves sting—cook, dry, or blend to deactivate hairs
- Avoid in pregnancy without guidance (root in particular)

Yarrow (Achillea millefolium)

Botanical Overview

- **Family:** Asteraceae
- **Parts Used:** Aerial parts (flowers, leaves)
- **Plant Type:** Perennial
- **Height:** 1–3 feet

YARROW

Botanical Features

- **Leaves:** Feathery, fern-like, soft and aromatic

- **Flowers:** Flat clusters of white, pink, or yellow blooms
- **Aroma:** Earthy and sweet with a bitter undertone

Growing & Harvesting

- Drought-tolerant; thrives in wild fields or gardens
- Harvest in bloom and dry quickly to retain oils

Medicinal Actions

- Astringent, styptic (stops bleeding), diaphoretic
- Used for wound healing, fever management, and menstrual support

⚠ Caution

- Avoid internal use during pregnancy
- May trigger allergies in sensitive individuals (daisy family)

Skullcap (Scutellaria lateriflora)

Botanical Overview

- **Family:** Lamiaceae (Mint family)
- **Parts Used:** Aerial parts (especially fresh)
- **Plant Type:** Perennial
- **Height:** 1–2 feet

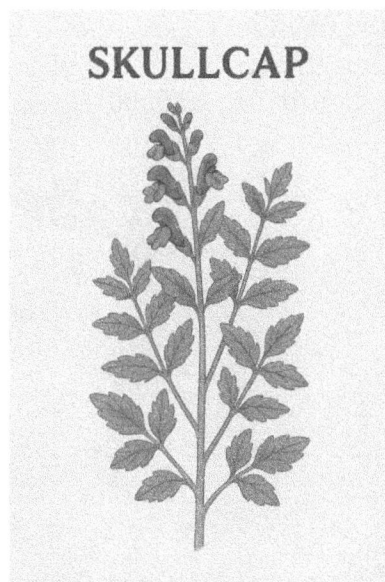

SKULLCAP

Botanical Features

- **Leaves:** Lance-shaped with jagged edges
- **Flowers:** Small blue-violet blooms in pairs
- **Growth Habit:** Upright, branching stems with a clean, mild scent

Growing & Harvesting

- Likes moist, shaded areas; often found near streams
- Harvest aerial parts before or during early flowering stage

Medicinal Actions

- Nervine, sedative, antispasmodic
- Eases nervous tension, muscle twitching, insomnia, and headaches

⚠ Caution

- Best used fresh or freshly dried for potency
- Do not confuse with other species (e.g., Baikal skullcap)

Tulsi (Ocimum sanctum / Ocimum tenuiflorum)

(Also known as Holy Basil)

Botanical Overview

- **Family:** Lamiaceae (Mint family)
- **Parts Used:** Leaves, stems, flowers
- **Plant Type:** Annual or short-lived perennial
- **Height:** 1–3 feet

TULSI
(HOLY BASIL)

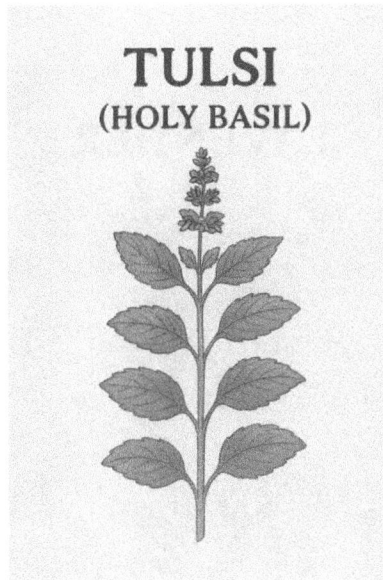

Botanical Features

- **Leaves:** Oval, slightly serrated, green or purplish depending on variety
- **Flowers:** Purple or white, arranged in upright spikes
- **Scent:** Spicy, clove-like aroma

Growing & Harvesting

- Loves warmth and sun; can be grown indoors or in pots
- Pinch back leaves regularly to encourage bushiness and flavor

Medicinal Actions

- Adaptogen, immune modulator, digestive aid
- Supports mood, stress resilience, respiratory function, and blood sugar balance

⚠ Caution

- Generally safe, though use cautiously in low blood sugar or with medication

Lavender (Lavandula angustifolia)

Botanical Overview

- **Family:** Lamiaceae (Mint family)
- **Parts Used:** Flowers
- **Plant Type:** Perennial, woody shrub

- **Height:** 1–3 feet

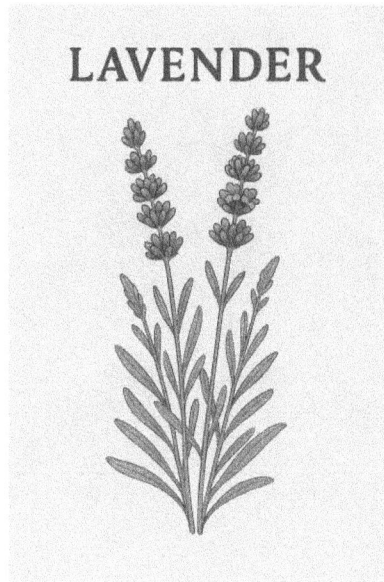

Botanical Features

- **Leaves:** Narrow, gray-green, fragrant when crushed
- **Flowers:** Small, violet to deep purple, arranged in spikes
- **Aroma:** Sweet, floral, calming

Growing & Harvesting

- Prefers full sun, dry conditions, and well-drained sandy soil
- Harvest flower spikes just as they begin to open for highest oil content
- Hang upside down in small bunches to dry

Medicinal Actions

- Calming nervine, antimicrobial, carminative
- Used for sleep, anxiety, digestive discomfort, and minor burns

⚠ Caution

- Strong scent; test before topical use if sensitive
- Internal use best in small amounts or as tea

Licorice Root (Glycyrrhiza glabra)

Botanical Overview

- **Family:** Fabaceae (Legume family)
- **Parts Used:** Root
- **Plant Type:** Perennial
- **Height:** 3–5 feet

LICORICE ROOT

Botanical Features

- **Leaves:** Pinnate (feather-like), with 9–17 small leaflets
- **Flowers:** Pale blue or purple, pea-shaped
- **Root:** Long, sweet-tasting, fibrous taproot

Growing & Harvesting

- Thrives in full sun and loamy soil; requires patience (3 years to mature)
- Harvest in fall, wash thoroughly, and slice to dry

Medicinal Actions

- Demulcent, anti-inflammatory, adrenal tonic
- Used for sore throats, ulcers, fatigue, and respiratory conditions

⚠ Caution

- Avoid prolonged use in high doses—it can raise blood pressure
- Choose **deglycyrrhizinated licorice (DGL)** if you're sensitive or hypertensive

Dandelion (Taraxacum officinale)

Botanical Overview

- **Family:** Asteraceae
- **Parts Used:** Root, leaf, flower
- **Plant Type:** Perennial weed/herb
- **Height:** 6–12 inches

DANDELION

Botanical Features

- **Leaves:** Deeply toothed, basal rosette
- **Flowers:** Bright yellow, composite, appear in early spring
- **Roots:** Long taproot, beige on outside, white inside

Growing & Harvesting

- Found abundantly in lawns, gardens, roadsides
- Harvest **roots in fall**, **leaves in spring**, and **flowers in bloom**

Medicinal Actions

- Diuretic, liver tonic, bitter
- Leaves used for water retention and potassium replenishment
- Root used to support liver, digestion, and detoxification

⚠ Caution

- Make sure it's grown away from pesticides and road pollution

- May aggravate bile duct or gallbladder conditions

Burdock Root (Arctium lappa)

Botanical Overview

- **Family:** Asteraceae
- **Parts Used:** Root, seed
- **Plant Type:** Biennial
- **Height:** Up to 5–6 feet

Botanical Features

- **Leaves:** Large, heart-shaped, fuzzy on underside
- **Flowers:** Purple thistle-like balls with burrs
- **Root:** Long, beige to brown taproot with earthy smell

Growing & Harvesting

- Harvest root in **first-year fall** or **second-year spring** before flowering
- Grows wild in fields, meadows, roadsides

Medicinal Actions

- Blood purifier, lymphatic, liver detoxifier
- Supports skin health (acne, eczema), digestion, and mild diuresis

⚠ Caution

- Large roots are hard to dig; consider gloves due to burrs
- May lower blood sugar—monitor if diabetic

Plantain Leaf (Plantago major / lanceolata)

Botanical Overview

- **Family:** Plantaginaceae
- **Parts Used:** Leaves
- **Plant Type:** Perennial herb
- **Height:** 4–12 inches

Botanical Features

- **Leaves:** Oval (P. major) or lance-shaped (P. lanceolata), with visible parallel veins
- **Flowers:** Long spikes with small green flowers
- **Texture:** Slightly chewy, mucilaginous when crushed

Growing & Harvesting

- Grows in lawns, sidewalks, trails (often stepped on!)
- Harvest young, clean leaves in spring and summer

Medicinal Actions

- Vulnerary, anti-inflammatory, demulcent
- Used for insect bites, skin irritation, and wound healing
- Internally supports digestive tract lining and cough relief

⚠ Caution

- Safe for most people, even children
- Avoid plants near traffic or pollution

Mullein (Verbascum thapsus)

Botanical Overview

- **Family:** Scrophulariaceae
- **Parts Used:** Leaves, flowers, root (occasionally)
- **Plant Type:** Biennial
- **Height:** 2–6 feet

Botanical Features

- **Leaves:** Large, thick, velvety, gray-green; rosette shape in year 1
- **Flowers:** Tall yellow flowering spike in year 2
- **Stem:** Woolly, upright, often central stalk

Growing & Harvesting

- Prefers dry, open areas with poor soil (roadsides, meadows)
- Harvest **leaves in first year**, **flowers in second** when freshly open

Medicinal Actions

- Expectorant, demulcent, anti-inflammatory
- Soothes dry cough, supports lung health, and eases earaches (flowers)

⚠ Caution

- Fine hairs on leaves can irritate throat—strain tea well
- Use only dried flowers/leaves internally

Marshmallow Root (Althaea officinalis)

Botanical Overview

- **Family:** Malvaceae
- **Parts Used:** Root, leaves
- **Plant Type:** Perennial
- **Height:** 3–5 feet

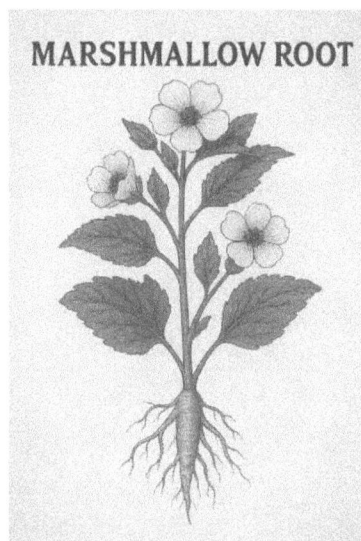

MARSHMALLOW ROOT

Botanical Features

- **Leaves:** Soft, velvety, 3-lobed and pale green
- **Flowers:** Pale pink or white, hibiscus-like
- **Root:** Thick, starchy, white interior with mucilage

Growing & Harvesting

- Prefers moist soils and full to partial sun
- Harvest **roots in fall**, **leaves in summer**—clean and dry gently

Medicinal Actions

- Demulcent, emollient, soothing
- Used for dry cough, sore throat, digestive inflammation, and urinary tract irritation

⚠ Caution

- May interfere with absorption of medications—space out doses
- Best taken cold-infused to preserve mucilage properties

Sage (Salvia officinalis)

Botanical Overview

- **Family:** Lamiaceae (Mint family)
- **Parts Used:** Leaves
- **Plant Type:** Perennial woody herb
- **Height:** 1–3 feet

SAGE

Botanical Features

- **Leaves:** Soft, gray-green, oval, aromatic and fuzzy
- **Flowers:** Purple-blue, in whorls along spikes
- **Scent:** Pungent and earthy, especially when rubbed

Growing & Harvesting

- Likes full sun and well-drained soil
- Harvest leaves before flowering for best flavor and oil content

Medicinal Actions

- Antimicrobial, astringent, hormone-regulating
- Useful for sore throats, excessive sweating, and menopausal hot flashes

⚠ Caution

- Avoid large internal doses during pregnancy or nursing
- Strong flavor—use sparingly in tea blends

Thyme (Thymus vulgaris)

Botanical Overview

- **Family:** Lamiaceae (Mint family)
- **Parts Used:** Leaves and flowering tops

- **Plant Type:** Perennial herb (evergreen in warm climates)
- **Height:** 6–12 inches

THYME

Botanical Features

- **Leaves:** Small, oval, grey-green, aromatic
- **Flowers:** Tiny, pink to purple, in dense clusters
- **Scent:** Warm, pungent, earthy with subtle lemony tones

Growing & Harvesting

- Thrives in full sun, well-drained soil—tolerates drought
- Harvest in late morning when oils are most concentrated
- Use fresh or dry for long-term storage

Medicinal Actions

- Antimicrobial, antispasmodic, expectorant
- Traditionally used for respiratory infections, coughs, digestion, and skin support
- Supports immune function and gut health

⚠ Caution

- Use essential oil with caution—always dilute
- High doses may irritate mucous membranes or cause sensitivity in some individuals

Rosemary (Rosmarinus officinalis)

Botanical Overview

- **Family:** Lamiaceae
- **Parts Used:** Leaves
- **Plant Type:** Evergreen shrub (in warm climates)
- **Height:** 2–6 feet

Botanical Features

- **Leaves:** Needle-like, dark green on top, silvery underside
- **Flowers:** Blue or lavender, small, lip-shaped
- **Scent:** Strong, piney, and invigorating

Growing & Harvesting

- Prefers full sun, sandy soil, and good drainage
- Harvest leaves year-round; dry or infuse fresh

Medicinal Actions

- Circulatory stimulant, memory aid, antioxidant
- Used for improving concentration, scalp health, and digestive support

⚠ Caution

- Avoid high internal doses in pregnancy
- Strong oil—dilute when using topically

Catnip (Nepeta cataria)

Botanical Overview

- **Family:** Lamiaceae (Mint family)
- **Parts Used:** Leaves, flowering tops
- **Plant Type:** Perennial
- **Height:** 2–3 feet

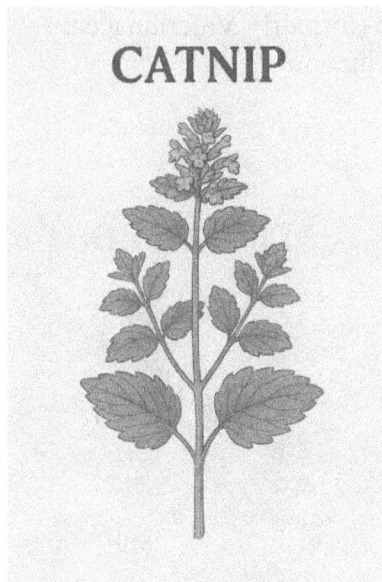

Botanical Features

- **Leaves:** Heart-shaped, soft, and fuzzy with serrated edges
- **Flowers:** Small, white to lavender, arranged in spikes
- **Scent:** Strongly minty and slightly skunky to humans; intoxicating to cats

Growing & Harvesting

- Easy to grow in sun or partial shade; repels insects
- Harvest before full bloom for peak potency; dry gently

Medicinal Actions

- Gentle sedative, antispasmodic, mild digestive aid
- Used for children's colic, restlessness, fevers, and mild anxiety

⚠ Caution

- Overuse may cause drowsiness
- May attract neighborhood cats if grown outdoors!

Valerian Root (Valeriana officinalis)

Botanical Overview

- **Family:** Caprifoliaceae (formerly Valerianaceae)
- **Parts Used:** Root and rhizome
- **Plant Type:** Perennial
- **Height:** 3–5 feet

Botanical Features

- **Leaves:** Pinnate, deeply divided; grow in whorls up the stem
- **Flowers:** Tiny, pale pink or white clusters with sweet scent
- **Root:** Thick, knobby, with strong earthy smell (often compared to old cheese or socks)

Growing & Harvesting

- Likes damp soil and partial sun; allow 2–3 years before harvesting root
- Uproot in fall, clean well, and dry thoroughly

Medicinal Actions

- Potent sedative, muscle relaxant, nervine
- Used for insomnia, anxiety, tension, and menstrual cramps

⚠ Caution

- May cause vivid dreams or grogginess in some
- Avoid alcohol and driving after use

Passionflower (Passiflora incarnata)

Botanical Overview

- **Family:** Passifloraceae
- **Parts Used:** Aerial parts (leaves, stems, flowers)
- **Plant Type:** Perennial climbing vine
- **Height:** Can grow over 10 feet with support

PASSIONFLOWER

Botanical Features

- **Leaves:** Lobed, deep green, tendril-bearing
- **Flowers:** Intricate, purple and white, with a distinctive corona

- **Fruit:** Small and round (edible but not the main medicinal part)

Growing & Harvesting

- Prefers warm climates and sun; needs a trellis or fence
- Harvest when in full bloom; dry in thin layers away from sun

Medicinal Actions

- Nervine, sedative, antispasmodic
- Helps quiet a busy mind, reduce racing thoughts, and support restful sleep

⚠ Caution

- Not recommended during pregnancy
- May increase effects of sedative medications

Red Clover (Trifolium pratense)

Botanical Overview

- **Family:** Fabaceae (Legume family)
- **Parts Used:** Blossoms (flowers)
- **Plant Type:** Biennial or short-lived perennial
- **Height:** 1–2 feet

RED CLOVER

Botanical Features

- **Leaves:** Trifoliate (three-part) with a pale chevron on each leaflet
- **Flowers:** Round, pinkish-purple globes made of many tiny flowers
- **Scent:** Mildly sweet and grassy when fresh

Growing & Harvesting

- Found in meadows and lawns; attracts bees
- Pick flowers in full bloom, avoiding browning heads; dry carefully

Medicinal Actions

- Blood purifier, lymphatic, mild phytoestrogenic effects
- Used for skin conditions, menopausal support, and detoxification

⚠ Caution

- May thin the blood—use caution if on anticoagulants
- Avoid during pregnancy due to estrogenic properties

Cleavers (Galium aparine)

(Also known as Goosegrass or Stickyweed)

Botanical Overview

- **Family:** Rubiaceae
- **Parts Used:** Aerial parts
- **Plant Type:** Annual vine
- **Height:** 1–3 feet (sprawling habit)

CLEAVERS

Botanical Features

- **Leaves:** Whorled (in circles), narrow, slightly sticky
- **Stems:** Covered in tiny hooked hairs, cling to clothes and fur
- **Flowers:** Tiny, white or greenish, grow from leaf axils

Growing & Harvesting

- Grows prolifically in spring along fence lines, gardens, wood edges
- Best used fresh, or freeze if needed—doesn't dry well

Medicinal Actions

- Lymphatic cleanser, diuretic, cooling
- Supports swollen lymph nodes, skin eruptions, and urinary tract

⚠ Caution

- Gentle and safe, though best used fresh for medicinal potency
- Not typically used in pregnancy due to diuretic action

Horsetail (Equisetum arvense)

(Also called Shavegrass)

Botanical Overview

- **Family:** Equisetaceae
- **Parts Used:** Sterile green stems

- **Plant Type:** Perennial fern ally
- **Height:** 1–2 feet

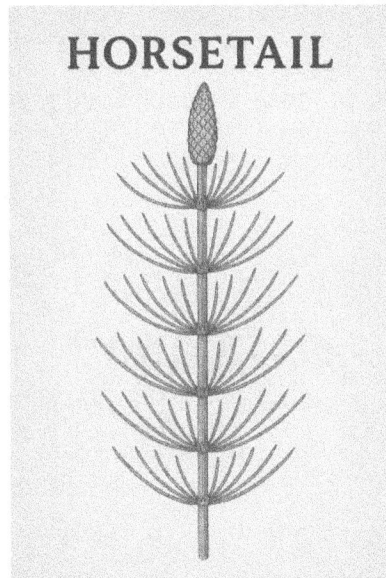

HORSETAIL

Botanical Features

- **Appearance:** Hollow, jointed stems resembling asparagus or bamboo
- **Leaves:** Needle-like whorls at stem joints
- **Texture:** Rough due to high silica content (like fine sandpaper)

Growing & Harvesting

- Prefers moist environments like streambanks or ditches
- Harvest green stems in spring/early summer before browning; dry quickly

Medicinal Actions

- Diuretic, mineral-rich (especially silica), astringent
- Supports bone, hair, nails, urinary tract, and connective tissues

⚠ Caution

- Avoid long-term use internally due to thiaminase (can deplete B1)
- Only use **Equisetum arvense** – other species can be toxic

Oatstraw (Avena sativa)

Botanical Overview

- **Family:** Poaceae (Grass family)
- **Parts Used:** Aerial parts in milky stage or dried green stems
- **Plant Type:** Annual grain crop
- **Height:** 2–4 feet

Botanical Features

- **Stems/Leaves:** Long, narrow grass blades
- **Seed Heads:** Pale green in early stages, mature to oat grains
- **Texture:** Soft, slightly grassy when fresh; dry for tea

Growing & Harvesting

- Grows easily in temperate regions, like wheat or barley
- Harvest tops when seeds exude a white "milk" when pressed

Medicinal Actions

- Nervine, nutritive, restorative
- Rebuilds the nervous system, especially after burnout or stress

- Very safe, even for children
- Some individuals with gluten intolerance may be sensitive—though oats are naturally gluten-free, contamination can occur

Ashwagandha (Withania somnifera)

(Known as Indian Ginseng)

Botanical Overview

- **Family:** Solanaceae (Nightshade family)
- **Parts Used:** Root
- **Plant Type:** Perennial shrub in warm climates (annual in temperate zones)
- **Height:** 1–3 feet

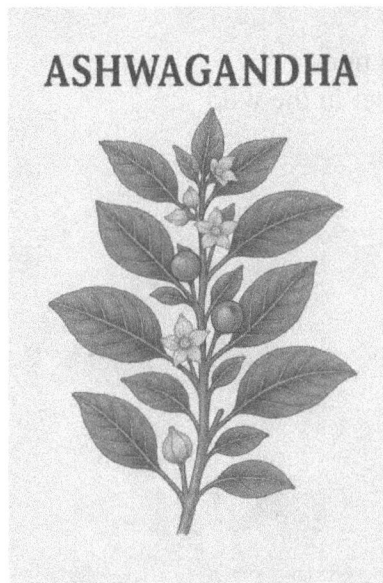

Botanical Features

- **Leaves:** Oval, dull green, lightly fuzzy
- **Flowers:** Greenish-yellow, small, bell-shaped
- **Fruit:** Small, red, enclosed in a papery husk (like a ground cherry)

Growing & Harvesting

- Likes full sun and sandy soil; needs a long growing season

- Roots harvested in fall; dry well and store in powder or whole form

Medicinal Actions

- Adaptogen, anti-stress, mild sedative
- Supports adrenal health, stamina, thyroid function, and sleep quality

⚠ Caution

- Avoid during pregnancy unless supervised by a professional
- Belongs to the nightshade family – use cautiously in sensitive individuals

Cinnamon (Cinnamomum verum / C. cassia)

Botanical Overview

- **Family:** Lauraceae
- **Parts Used:** Inner bark
- **Plant Type:** Evergreen tree
- **Height:** Up to 30–40 feet in the wild

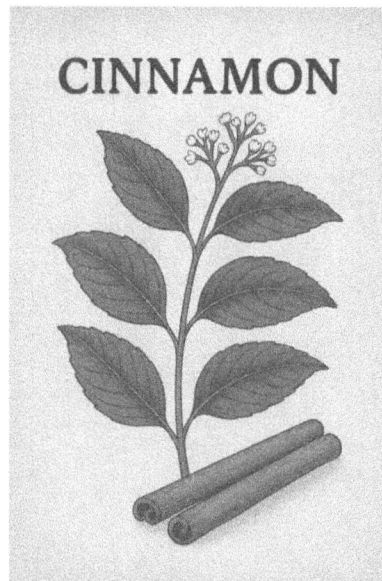

Botanical Features

- **Leaves:** Oval, leathery, with prominent veins
- **Bark:** Brown-gray outer bark; inner bark is fragrant and curls into quills when dried
- **Aroma:** Sweet, spicy, warm

Growing & Harvesting

- Cultivated in tropical regions (Sri Lanka, India, etc.)
- Bark is stripped from branches and dried into sticks or powdered

Medicinal Actions

- Warming stimulant, antimicrobial, carminative
- Helps regulate blood sugar, aid digestion, and improve circulation

⚠ Caution

- **Cassia cinnamon** (common grocery type) contains more coumarin—can be liver-toxic in large doses
- Use **Ceylon cinnamon (C. verum)** for safer long-term use

Fennel (Foeniculum vulgare)

Botanical Overview

- **Family:** Apiaceae (Carrot family)
- **Parts Used:** Seeds, bulb, leaves
- **Plant Type:** Perennial (grown as annual in some climates)
- **Height:** 3–5 feet

FENNEL

Botanical Features

- **Leaves:** Feathery, dill-like fronds
- **Flowers:** Umbels of tiny yellow blossoms
- **Seeds:** Small, oblong, aromatic (actually a fruit technically)

Growing & Harvesting

- Likes full sun and rich soil
- Seeds harvested in late summer when dry; leaves and bulbs can be used fresh

Medicinal Actions

- Carminative, antispasmodic, mild estrogenic
- Used for gas, bloating, colic (in infants), and supporting lactation

⚠ Caution

- Avoid concentrated doses during pregnancy
- Use seed form rather than essential oil internally unless supervised

Milk Thistle (Silybum marianum)

Botanical Overview

- **Family:** Asteraceae
- **Parts Used:** Seeds (occasionally leaves)
- **Plant Type:** Annual or biennial
- **Height:** 3–5 feet

MILK THISTLE

Botanical Features

- **Leaves:** Shiny, green with white marbling and spiny edges
- **Flowers:** Large, thistle-like, purple-pink blooms
- **Seeds:** Small, brown, and hard—contained in the flower head after blooming

Growing & Harvesting

- Prefers sunny, dry locations and poor soil
- Seeds are collected in late summer when heads dry and turn brown

Medicinal Actions

- Hepatoprotective, antioxidant, regenerative
- Supports liver detox, regeneration, and protection from toxins or medications

⚠ Caution

- May interact with medications metabolized by the liver
- Use seeds, not other parts, for liver-specific action

Goldenseal (Hydrastis canadensis)

Botanical Overview

- **Family:** Ranunculaceae (Buttercup family)
- **Parts Used:** Root and rhizome
- **Plant Type:** Perennial woodland herb
- **Height:** 6–12 inches

GOLDENSEAL

Botanical Features

- **Leaves:** Broad, palmate, wrinkled with 5 lobes
- **Flowers:** Greenish-white, small, without petals
- **Root:** Bright yellow and knobby; contains berberine (active compound)

Growing & Harvesting

- Native to shady, moist forests in North America
- Harvest in fall of the 3rd year; drying must be done carefully

Medicinal Actions

- Antimicrobial, bitter tonic, mucous membrane restorative
- Used for infections (especially respiratory and digestive), mouth ulcers, and gut inflammation

⚠ Caution

- Overharvested in the wild—buy cultivated or organic only
- Avoid during pregnancy or if using strong medications

Blue Vervain (Verbena hastata)

Botanical Overview

- **Family:** Verbenaceae
- **Parts Used:** Aerial parts (flowers, leaves)
- **Plant Type:** Perennial wildflower
- **Height:** 3–5 feet

BLUE VERVAIN

Botanical Features

- **Leaves:** Lance-shaped with serrated edges, rough texture
- **Flowers:** Spiky purple-blue florets arranged in branched clusters
- **Growth Habit:** Upright, narrow, often found in damp areas

Growing & Harvesting

- Prefers moist meadows, streamsides, and open woodlands
- Harvest before full flowering; dry in shade quickly

Medicinal Actions

- Nervine, bitter tonic, antispasmodic
- Used to calm nervous tension, especially with headaches or menstrual imbalance

⚠ Caution

- Very bitter—best taken in tincture or capsule if taste is an issue
- Not for use in pregnancy due to uterine stimulating properties

Garlic (Allium sativum)

Botanical Overview

- **Family:** Amaryllidaceae
- **Parts Used:** Bulb (cloves)
- **Plant Type:** Perennial (grown as annual)
- **Height:** 1–2 feet

Botanical Features

- **Leaves:** Flat, grass-like
- **Flowers:** Small white or purple blooms on a tall stalk (scape)
- **Bulb:** Made of multiple papery-wrapped cloves beneath the soil

Growing & Harvesting

- Plant in fall for summer harvest; likes full sun and rich, loose soil
- Harvest when lower leaves yellow; dry in cool, dark place

Medicinal Actions

- Antimicrobial, circulatory stimulant, immune-enhancing
- Used for colds, infections, heart health, and general immune support

⚠ Caution

- Can irritate the stomach in large doses
- Raw garlic is more potent but also harsher; use wisely

Slippery Elm (Ulmus rubra)

Botanical Overview

- **Family:** Ulmaceae
- **Parts Used:** Inner bark
- **Plant Type:** Deciduous tree
- **Height:** Up to 60–80 feet

SLIPPERY ELM

Botanical Features

- **Leaves:** Large, rough, toothed with asymmetrical bases
- **Bark:** Outer bark dark and furrowed; inner bark is soft, mucilaginous when moist
- **Flowers:** Small, red, appear before leaves

Growing & Harvesting

- Inner bark harvested in early spring; only from fallen or pruned limbs (to protect the tree)
- Bark is dried and powdered

Medicinal Actions

- Demulcent, emollient, anti-inflammatory
- Soothes sore throats, ulcers, acid reflux, and irritated digestive lining

⚠ Caution

- Best used in powder or lozenge form
- Ethical sourcing is crucial—slippery elm trees are threatened in some areas

Comfrey (Symphytum officinale)

(Also known as Knitbone)

Botanical Overview

- **Family:** Boraginaceae
- **Parts Used:** Leaves and roots
- **Plant Type:** Perennial herb
- **Height:** 2–4 feet

COMFREY

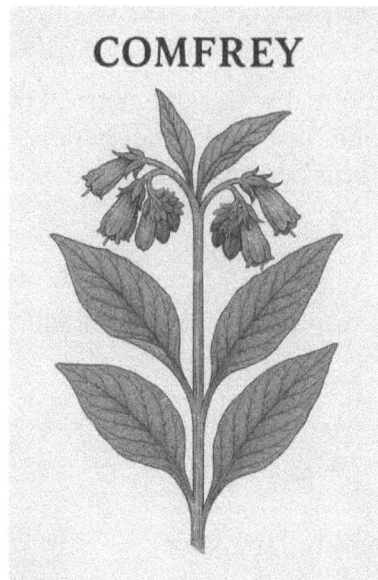

Botanical Features

- **Leaves:** Large, lance-shaped, rough and hairy
- **Flowers:** Bell-shaped, purple or cream-colored
- **Roots:** Black on the outside, white and mucilaginous inside

Growing & Harvesting

- Thrives in moist, rich soils and partial shade
- Harvest leaves before flowering; roots in fall of 2nd year
- Very fast-growing and self-spreading

Medicinal Actions

- Cell proliferant, wound healer, demulcent
- Traditionally used externally for sprains, bruises, broken bones, and ulcers

⚠ Caution

- Internal use discouraged due to **pyrrolizidine alkaloids (PAs)** which can be toxic to the liver
- Safe for **external** use only—avoid open wounds or prolonged use

Chickweed (Stellaria media)

Botanical Overview

- **Family:** Caryophyllaceae

- **Parts Used:** Aerial parts (fresh preferred)
- **Plant Type:** Low-growing annual
- **Height:** Up to 6 inches

CHICKWEED

Botanical Features

- **Leaves:** Small, oval, opposite with smooth edges
- **Stems:** Delicate, with a single line of fine hairs
- **Flowers:** Tiny white star-shaped blooms with deeply cleft petals

Growing & Harvesting

- Common in cool seasons, gardens, and lawns
- Harvest young before flowering; use fresh or lightly wilted

Medicinal Actions

- Cooling, demulcent, anti-inflammatory
- Used topically for itchy skin, eczema, rashes, and internally for soothing digestion

⚠ Caution

- Very safe for internal or external use
- Must be used **fresh or freshly prepared** to retain potency

Black Cohosh (Actaea racemosa)

(Formerly Cimicifuga racemosa)

Botanical Overview

- **Family:** Ranunculaceae (Buttercup family)
- **Parts Used:** Root and rhizome
- **Plant Type:** Tall woodland perennial
- **Height:** 4–6 feet

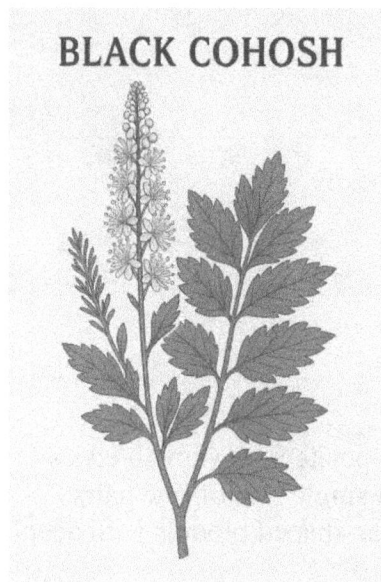

BLACK COHOSH

Botanical Features

- **Leaves:** Large, compound, with serrated edges
- **Flowers:** Tall white plume-like spikes with no petals; fragrant
- **Root:** Thick, knotty, and brown

Growing & Harvesting

- Prefers shaded woodlands and moist soil
- Root harvested in fall of 3rd year; sustainable cultivation is encouraged

Medicinal Actions

- Antispasmodic, hormone modulator, nervine
- Used for menopausal symptoms (hot flashes, mood swings), PMS, and uterine cramping

- Do not use during pregnancy without guidance
- Avoid in liver disorders or with estrogen-sensitive conditions

Hibiscus (Hibiscus sabdariffa)

(Also called Roselle)

Botanical Overview

- **Family:** Malvaceae
- **Parts Used:** Calyx (outer part of the flower), occasionally leaves
- **Plant Type:** Annual or perennial (tropical zones)
- **Height:** 3–7 feet

HIBISCUS

Botanical Features

- **Leaves:** Deep green, lobed with red stems
- **Flowers:** Bright red to deep pink calyces with fleshy texture
- **Flavor:** Tart, cranberry-like when steeped

Growing & Harvesting

- Loves warm climates and full sun
- Harvest calyces after flowering when plump and red

Medicinal Actions

- Cooling, antioxidant, hypotensive
- Excellent for blood pressure regulation, kidney support, and cooling inflammation

⚠ Caution

- May lower blood pressure—monitor if on BP medication
- Strongly cooling—balance with warming herbs if needed

Common Pairings & Blends

- **Stress relief**: Lemon balm + lavender + chamomile
- **Immune support**: Elderberry + echinacea + ginger
- **Digestion**: Peppermint + fennel + ginger
- **Sleep blend**: Passionflower + skullcap + valerian root
- **Detox and liver support**: Dandelion root + burdock + red clover

💡 Tip: Start with a few herbs that support **your most common needs**, like better sleep, immune defense, or digestion.

Where to Buy Quality Herbs and Supplies

- **Reputable online apothecaries**:
    - Mountain Rose Herbs
    - Starwest Botanicals
    - Frontier Co-op
- **Local sources**:
    - Herb farms
    - Farmers' markets
    - Natural food stores with bulk herb sections

Always check for organic certifications, harvest dates, and whether herbs are wildcrafted, cultivated, or imported. Look for freshness—good herbs smell fragrant and look vibrant.

Chapter 6

Setting Up Your Apothecary Space

Creating a functional and inspiring herbal workspace makes practicing herbalism easier, safer, and more enjoyable. Whether you have a dedicated shelf, kitchen cabinet, or full home studio, a little organization goes a long way.

Organizing Your Herbs and Tools

- Use **clear glass jars** for visibility and beauty.
- Arrange by **alphabet**, **remedy type**, or **body system** (e.g., respiratory, digestive).

- Keep your most-used tools (strainers, droppers, jars) in a designated drawer or tray.
- Hang drying herbs on hooks, rods, or racks in a warm, dry place.

Labeling, Dating & Inventory

Every container should include:

- Herb name and part used (e.g., Calendula flowers)
- Date harvested or purchased
- Source: wildcrafted, organic, garden-grown
- Intended use or batch info (e.g., "Cold remedy tincture #2")

Use a **simple spreadsheet or notebook** to keep track of what you have, what's running low, and expiration dates.

Keeping a Herbal Journal or Remedy Log

Your herbal journal is your **personal materia medica**. Use it to:

- Track recipes, dosages, outcomes
- Note herbal observations—taste, smell, effect, preparation methods
- Record family health notes or seasonal formulas
- Sketch plants or paste pressed flowers
- Track gardening successes and wild foraging experiences

Over time, your journal becomes a **legacy document**—a personal, evolving archive of healing knowledge that's rooted in your lived experience.

===============Break in Transmission===========

Permit me to take a brief pause right here to ask for a favor. If you have found the first few chapters of this book insightful and helpful to you, kindly leave an honest on my book page. Reviews encourage other readers to give independent authors like myself a chance to be heard. Trust me, it sure helps.

Thank you!

Moving on…

Chapter 7

Herbal Teas & Infusions

"A cup of tea is a cup of peace." – Soshitsu Sen XV

Tea is more than a warm drink. In herbalism, it's a **gentle yet profound form of medicine**, offering the body nutrients, plant compounds, and comfort in every sip. Herbal teas and infusions are **foundational to any home apothecary** because they are easy to prepare, affordable, and versatile—and perhaps most importantly, they make herbal healing **accessible to everyone**, from beginner to seasoned herbalist.

This chapter will teach you not only how to make teas and infusions, but also **how to think like a tea-formulating herbalist**, empowering you to blend for **mood, digestion, immunity, energy, and beyond**.

What's the Difference Between Tea and Infusion?

- **Herbal Tea**: A quick brew using soft plant parts—leaves, flowers, and delicate stems—steeped in hot water for 5–15 minutes. Light and fragrant.
- **Infusion**: A **stronger, medicinal version** of tea, steeped for several hours or overnight, often using larger amounts of herbs to extract more vitamins, minerals, and bioactive compounds.

✦ *Tip: Think of a tea as a quick comfort drink, and an infusion as a daily health tonic.*

The Art of Blending Medicinal Teas

A powerful herbal tea isn't just about what tastes good. It's about **formulating with purpose**. Herbal tea blends often use a three-part structure:

1. Base Herbs – for volume and nourishment

These make up the bulk of the blend and offer deep nutrition or balancing properties. *Examples*: Nettle, oatstraw, red clover, raspberry leaf

2. Supporting Herbs – for therapeutic action

These target specific systems (digestion, sleep, lungs) and direct the purpose of the blend. *Examples*: Chamomile (calming), fennel (digestive), elderflower (immune support)

3. Accent Herbs – for flavor, aroma, and personality

A small percentage, added for their brightness or to enhance taste and harmony. *Examples*: Cinnamon, licorice, rose petals, cardamom

💡 *Blending is both science and art. Don't worry if your first attempt isn't perfect—your taste buds are your best guide.*

Sleep, Digestion, Immunity, Energy

In herbalism, one of the simplest yet most powerful ways to experience plant medicine is through **teas and infusions**. When chosen with intention, a warm cup of herbal tea can calm the nervous system, soothe digestive upsets, boost immunity, or gently uplift energy—naturally and without side effects.

This section introduces how to work with herbs that support the body's foundational systems, helping you create nourishing daily rituals that bring your body into balance. Whether you're winding down for restful sleep, nurturing gut health, staying resilient during seasonal shifts, or looking for caffeine-free vitality—there's a plant-powered blend for you.

A comprehensive recipe section for targeted herbal teas and infusions follows this overview, offering easy, beginner-friendly preparations using the top herbs covered in this book.

Let's sip our way to wellness—one healing cup at a time. ☕

For Sleep and Calm

If your nervous system feels overworked or your mind won't slow down at bedtime, herbal teas can help support rest **without grogginess or dependency**.

Relaxation Tea Blend (1 cup)

- 1 tsp **Chamomile** – mild sedative, soothes anxiety
- 1 tsp **Lemon balm** – mood booster, calming
- ½ tsp **Passionflower** – promotes restful sleep
- Optional: ¼ tsp **Lavender** – aromatic and soothing

Steep for 10–15 minutes, inhale deeply before sipping. Drink 30–60 minutes before bedtime.

For Digestion

Digestive teas help reduce bloating, soothe cramps, and stimulate healthy enzyme production. These blends are perfect after meals or to calm an upset stomach.

Digestive Comfort Blend

- 1 tsp **Peppermint** – eases gas and spasms
- ½ tsp **Ginger root** – warms and stimulates digestion
- ½ tsp **Fennel seeds** – anti-gas, relieves indigestion
- ¼ tsp **Chamomile** – anti-inflammatory

Steep for 10–12 minutes. Sip slowly after eating.

⚠ *Avoid peppermint if you have acid reflux—it may relax the lower esophageal sphincter too much.*

For Immune Support

Immunity doesn't mean just "boosting"—it means **balancing and fortifying** the body so it can respond better to stress, viruses, and seasonal changes.

Cold Season Defender Tea

- 1 tsp **Elderflower** – opens sinuses, reduces fever
- 1 tsp **Yarrow** – stimulates circulation, immune support
- 1 tsp **Linden flower** – calming, diaphoretic
- Optional: ½ tsp **Licorice root** – anti-viral, harmonizer

Steep covered for 15 minutes. Sweeten with raw honey if desired and drink warm, 2–3 times daily at the first sign of illness.

For Energy & Focus

Unlike caffeine-driven energy, these teas **nourish and stimulate gently**, supporting long-term vitality without crashes.

Vitality Boosting Blend

- 1 tsp **Tulsi (Holy Basil)** – adaptogen, clears mental fog
- 1 tsp **Rosemary** – circulatory stimulant, aids memory
- 1 tsp **Lemon verbena** – uplifting and citrusy
- Optional: ½ tsp **Green tea** – mild caffeine (omit if avoiding stimulants)

Steep for 8–10 minutes. Enjoy as a morning pick-me-up or early afternoon "second wind" cup.

How to Brew the Perfect Cup

Preparation	Method
Standard Herbal Tea	1–2 tsp dried herbs / cup, steep in covered mug for 10–15 minutes
Infusion (strong tea)	1 oz dried herb (by weight) per quart of hot water, steep 4–8 hours
Cold Infusion (for mucilaginous herbs like marshmallow)	Steep in room-temp water 4–12 hrs
Straining	Use fine mesh strainer or muslin bag
Storing	Freshly brewed teas: drink within 24 hrs; infusions: refrigerate 2–3 days

Always cover your tea while steeping to trap the volatile essential oils—these carry the aromatic, calming, and antimicrobial properties.

Storage Tips

- **Keep dried herbs** in airtight glass jars, away from direct light or moisture.
- Label with the herb name and date.
- Use within 6–12 months for maximum potency and flavor.

Herbal Teas as Daily Ritual

Creating tea time isn't just about physical benefits—it's about forming a **habit of mindful healing**. Your tea ritual can become a moment of calm, presence, and connection with the earth.

"When we drink a tea made from dandelion, we are drinking the strength of persistence. When we sip chamomile, we are steeping in peace."

Sample 7-Day Tea Plan

Day	Morning	Evening
Mon	Vitality Boost Blend	Sleepy Chamomile Infusion
Tue	Tulsi + Peppermint	Lemon Balm + Passionflower
Wed	Nettle + Rosemary	Oatstraw + Lavender
Thu	Green Tea + Lemon Verbena	Chamomile + Catnip
Fri	Fennel + Licorice Root	Valerian + Skullcap
Sat	Digestive Comfort Tea	Nervine Nourish Blend
Sun	Cleavers + Red Clover	Raspberry Leaf + Rose

30 Medicinal Tea Blends

Practical Recipes to Support Body, Mind & Spirit—One Cup at a Time

Whether you're looking to calm anxiety, soothe a cough, boost your energy, or simply sip something nourishing, these carefully curated tea blends offer a reliable and natural way to support your health. Each recipe below is balanced for both **flavor and function**, keeping beginner accessibility and botanical effectiveness in mind.

Calming & Sleep Support

These blends are formulated to relax the nervous system, reduce anxiety, and promote restful sleep.

Sleepy Time Calm

Ingredients:

- 1 tsp Chamomile
- 1 tsp Lemon Balm
- ½ tsp Passionflower
- Pinch of Lavender

Instructions

Combine all herbs in a mug and pour over 8 oz of freshly boiled water. Cover and steep for 10–15 minutes. Strain and sip slowly.

Precautions:

- Avoid passionflower during pregnancy.
- Lavender may cause drowsiness in some people.

Dosage/Use:

Drink 1 cup 30–60 minutes before bedtime.

Nervine Nourish Tea

Ingredients:

- 1 tsp Oatstraw
- 1 tsp Skullcap
- ½ tsp Rose petals

Instructions

Steep the herbs in a covered mug of hot water for 15 minutes. Strain and enjoy warm or at room temperature.

Precautions:

- Oatstraw may cause issues for those with oat allergies.
- Skullcap may interact with sedatives.

Dosage/Use:

Drink 1–2 cups daily to nourish and calm the nervous system.

Deep Dream Blend

Ingredients:

- 1 tsp Valerian root
- 1 tsp Lemon Verbena
- ½ tsp Catnip

Instructions

Steep all herbs in hot water for 10–15 minutes with the mug covered. Strain and sweeten if desired.

Precautions:

- Valerian may cause vivid dreams or grogginess in some. Use at night only.
- Not recommended for use with sedative medications.

Dosage/Use:

1 cup before bedtime, as needed for restful sleep.

Nerve Calm Evening Tea

Ingredients:

- 1 part skullcap
- 1 part chamomile
- 1 part lemon balm
- 1/2 part lavender

Instructions

Combine herbs and store in a dark jar. Steep 1–2 teaspoons in 1 cup hot water for 10–15 minutes. Strain and drink warm before bed.

Precautions:

- May cause drowsiness; avoid operating machinery afterward.

Dosage/Use:

Drink 1 cup 30–60 minutes before sleep.

Respiratory & Immune Defense

Support respiratory health and boost your body's natural defenses with these blends.

Elderflower Immuni-Tea

Ingredients:

- 1 tsp Elderflower
- 1 tsp Yarrow
- ½ tsp Peppermint

Instructions

Steep the herbs in a cup of just-boiled water for 15 minutes with the lid on. Strain and drink while warm.

Precautions:

- Avoid yarrow in pregnancy.
- Elderflower may lower blood sugar.

Dosage/Use:

Drink 1–3 cups daily at the first sign of a cold or flu.

Lung Support Blend

Ingredients:

- 1 tsp Mullein leaf
- 1 tsp Licorice root
- ½ tsp Thyme

Instructions

Simmer licorice and thyme in 8 oz water for 10 minutes. Remove from heat, add mullein, cover, and steep an additional 10 minutes. Strain through a fine mesh.

Precautions:

- Avoid licorice if you have high blood pressure.
- Mullein hairs may irritate if not strained thoroughly.

Dosage/Use:

Drink up to 2 cups per day for lung and respiratory support.

Soothing Lung & Respiratory Tea

Ingredients:
- 1 part mullein leaf
- 1 part licorice root
- 1 part thyme
- 1/2 part peppermint

Instructions

Mix all herbs and store in an airtight container. Use 1–2 teaspoons per cup of boiling water. Steep for 10–15 minutes, then strain.

Precautions:

- Licorice may raise blood pressure when used in excess or over long periods.

Dosage/Use:

Drink 2–3 cups daily during colds or respiratory discomfort.

Digestive Relief & Gut Harmony

These herbal blends soothe the digestive tract, reduce bloating, and improve gut function.

Digest-Ease Tea

Ingredients:

- 1 tsp Peppermint
- ½ tsp Fennel seed
- ½ tsp Chamomile

Instructions

Combine herbs in a mug. Pour over 8 oz hot water, cover, and steep for 10–12 minutes. Strain and sip after meals.

Precautions:

- Avoid peppermint with acid reflux.
- Fennel may affect hormone-sensitive conditions.

Dosage/Use:

1 cup after meals or as needed for digestive relief.

Ginger Spice Digestif

Ingredients:

- 1 tsp Ginger root
- ½ tsp Cinnamon chips
- ½ tsp Orange peel

Instructions

Simmer all ingredients in 1 cup of water for 10 minutes. Strain and sweeten with honey if desired.

Precautions:

- Ginger may warm the body and increase sweating.
- Avoid in large doses if taking blood thinners.

Dosage/Use:

1 cup after meals or when experiencing gas or bloating.

Energy & Clarity Support

These blends provide gentle, sustained energy and mental sharpness without the crash of caffeine.

Vital Uplift Blend

Ingredients:

- 1 tsp Tulsi (Holy Basil)
- ½ tsp Gotu Kola
- 1 tsp Rosemary

Instructions

Steep herbs in hot water for 10–12 minutes, covered. Strain and enjoy warm or cool.

Precautions:

- Gotu Kola may cause drowsiness in high doses.
- Avoid rosemary during pregnancy in medicinal quantities.

Dosage/Use:

Drink 1 cup in the morning or early afternoon for alertness.

Gentle Morning Tonic

Ingredients:

- 1 tsp Nettle leaf
- ½ tsp Oatstraw
- ½ tsp Spearmint

Instructions

Steep herbs in boiling water for 15 minutes. Strain and drink as a morning tea.

Precautions:

- Nettle may increase urination.
- Avoid if allergic to grasses.

Dosage/Use:

1–2 cups in the morning for natural energy.

Matcha Adaptogen Tea

Ingredients:

- ½ tsp Matcha green tea powder
- ½ tsp Ashwagandha root
- Pinch of Cardamom

Instructions

Steep ashwagandha root in simmering water for 10 mins. Whisk in matcha and cardamom. Optional: add honey.

Precautions:

- Ashwagandha may lower blood pressure or interact with thyroid meds.
- Contains caffeine.

Dosage/Use:

1 cup in the morning for physical and mental resilience.

Heart, Mood & Hormone Support

These blends soothe emotional tension, regulate hormones, and support heart-centered calm.

Rose Glow Tea

Ingredients:

- 1 tsp Rose petals
- 1 tsp Lemon Balm
- ½ tsp Hawthorn leaf & flower

Instructions

Steep in hot water for 10–15 minutes, covered. Strain and sip slowly.

Precautions:

- Hawthorn may interact with heart medications.
- Rose petals may thin blood slightly.

Dosage/Use:

1–2 cups daily as a mood and heart tonic.

Hormone Balance Brew

Ingredients:

- 1 tsp Raspberry leaf
- ½ tsp Vitex (Chasteberry)
- ½ tsp Licorice root

Instructions

Simmer vitex and licorice for 10 mins. Add raspberry leaf and steep an additional 10 mins.

Precautions:

- Avoid licorice in hypertension.
- Vitex may alter hormone levels.

Dosage/Use:

Drink 1 cup daily, particularly during the luteal phase (after ovulation).

Mood Mender Tea

Ingredients:

- 1 tsp St. John's Wort
- 1 tsp Tulsi
- ½ tsp Lavender

Instructions

Steep all herbs for 10 minutes in a covered mug. Strain and drink once cooled slightly.

Precautions:

- St. John's Wort interacts with many medications (antidepressants, birth control, etc.).
- Consult your healthcare provider before use.

Dosage/Use:

1 cup daily during times of emotional stress.

Detox & Cleanse Support

Gentle daily detox blends that support your liver, kidneys, skin, and lymphatic system.

Gentle Daily Detox

Ingredients:

- 1 tsp Dandelion leaf
- ½ tsp Red Clover
- ½ tsp Cleavers

Instructions

Steep herbs in hot water for 15 minutes. Strain and drink warm or cold.

Precautions:

- Red clover may act like estrogen.
- Dandelion may increase urination.

Dosage/Use:

Drink 1–2 cups daily for 2–3 weeks.

Liver Love Tea

Ingredients:

- 1 tsp Burdock root
- 1 tsp Dandelion root
- ½ tsp Ginger

Instructions:

Simmer all ingredients for 15–20 minutes. Strain and drink warm.

Precautions:

- Burdock may interact with diuretics or diabetes meds.
- Not for use if bile duct is obstructed.

Dosage/Use:

1 cup daily for up to 2 weeks.

Kidney Flush Blend

Ingredients:

- 1 tsp Nettle leaf
- 1 tsp Cornsilk
- ½ tsp Marshmallow leaf

Instructions

Steep in hot water for 15 minutes, covered. Strain well and sip throughout the day.

Precautions:

- Avoid with kidney disease unless under medical guidance.
- May increase urination.

Dosage/Use

Drink 1 cup 1–2x per day for gentle urinary support.

Gentle Liver & Skin Support Tea

Ingredients:

- 1 part dandelion root
- 1 part burdock root
- 1/2 part calendula flowers
- 1/2 part red clover blossoms

Instructions

Combine herbs and store in a dry jar. Simmer 1–2 teaspoons in 1.5 cups water for 15–20 minutes. Strain and enjoy warm.

Precautions:

- Avoid during pregnancy.
- Consult doctor if taking medications processed by the liver.

Dosage/Use:

Drink 1 cup daily for up to 3 weeks, followed by a break.

Women's Wellness

These herbal blends are designed to support the hormonal, reproductive, and emotional well-being of women at all stages of life—from menstruation to menopause.

Moon Cycle Tea

Ingredients:

- 1 tsp Raspberry leaf
- ½ tsp Cramp Bark
- ½ tsp Chamomile

Instructions

Combine herbs and steep in hot water for 15 minutes, covered. Strain and sip slowly.

Precautions:

- Cramp bark should be avoided during pregnancy unless under supervision.
- Chamomile may cause allergic reactions in people sensitive to ragweed.

Dosage/Use:

Drink 1–2 cups daily during the days leading up to and during your menstrual cycle.

Mother's Nettle Nourish

Ingredients:

- 1 tsp Nettle
- 1 tsp Oatstraw
- ½ tsp Rose petals

Instructions

Steep in just-boiled water for 15–20 minutes. Strain well.

Precautions:

- Nettle may increase urination.
- Use only organic rose petals free of pesticide residues.

Dosage/Use:

Drink 1 cup daily as a general mineral tonic for postpartum recovery or monthly cycle balance.

Menopause Comfort Tea

Ingredients:

- 1 tsp Sage leaf
- ½ tsp Licorice root
- ½ tsp Motherwort

Instructions

Simmer licorice root in 8 oz of water for 10 minutes. Add sage and motherwort; steep 10 minutes. Strain before drinking.

Precautions:

- Sage can be drying—avoid in cases of dryness-related conditions.
- Avoid licorice in high blood pressure or long-term use.

Dosage/Use:

1 cup in the morning and evening during hot flashes or hormonal shifts.

Hormone Balance Women's Tea

Ingredients:

- 1 part raspberry leaf
- 1 part nettle leaf
- 1/2 part vitex berries
- 1/2 part rose petals

Instructions

Mix and store herbs in a cool, dry container. Steep 1 tablespoon in 2 cups hot water for 10–15 minutes. Strain before drinking.

Precautions:

Do not use vitex while on hormonal birth control without guidance.

Dosage/Use:

Drink daily, especially during the second half of the menstrual cycle.

Brain & Nervous System Support

These formulas support cognition, reduce mental fatigue, and help manage daily stress without sedating the body.

Clarity & Focus Tea

Ingredients:

- 1 tsp Gotu Kola
- 1 tsp Peppermint
- ½ tsp Ginkgo biloba

Instructions

Steep all herbs in hot water for 10–12 minutes, covered. Strain and enjoy.

Precautions:

- Ginkgo may thin the blood—avoid with anticoagulants.
- Peppermint not recommended in acid reflux.

Dosage/Use:

Drink 1 cup mid-morning or before mentally demanding tasks.

Stress Relief Sipper

Ingredients:

- 1 tsp Lemon Balm
- 1 tsp Tulsi
- ½ tsp Rose petals

Instructions

Steep herbs in hot water for 15 minutes, covered. Strain and sip.

Precautions:

- Lemon balm may lower thyroid activity in large doses.
- Tulsi may slightly lower blood sugar or blood pressure.

Dosage/Use:

Enjoy 1–2 cups daily during times of stress or burnout.

Skin & Anti-Inflammatory Support

These blends support internal detox pathways that contribute to radiant, healthy skin and reduce systemic inflammation.

Clear Skin Brew

Ingredients:

- 1 tsp Burdock root
- 1 tsp Red Clover
- ½ tsp Calendula flowers

Instructions

Simmer burdock for 10 minutes, then add red clover and calendula. Steep an additional 10 minutes. Strain before drinking.

Precautions:

- Red clover has estrogen-like effects.
- Calendula should be avoided if allergic to daisies or marigolds.

Dosage/Use:

Drink 1–2 cups daily as part of a skin-cleansing protocol.

Inflammation Ease Tea

Ingredients:

- 1 tsp Turmeric root or powder
- ½ tsp Ginger root
- Pinch of Black Pepper

Instructions

Simmer turmeric and ginger in 8 oz water for 10–15 minutes. Add black pepper last. Strain and serve with a splash of milk or honey if desired.

Precautions:

- Avoid turmeric in gallbladder disease.
- May stain teeth or mugs—use with care.

Dosage/Use:

Drink 1 cup 1–2 times daily to reduce systemic inflammation.

Immune & Vitality Support

Designed for general wellness, these blends offer gentle daily nourishment and promote resilience during times of stress or immune vulnerability.

Daily Vital Brew

Ingredients:

- 1 tsp Nettle leaf
- 1 tsp Red Clover
- ½ tsp Astragalus root

Instructions

Simmer astragalus root in 1 cup of water for 15 minutes. Add nettle and red clover, steep an additional 10 minutes covered. Strain.

Precautions:

- Avoid during acute illness (astragalus is for prevention, not active infection).

- Red clover may interact with blood-thinning medications.

Dosage/Use:

1 cup daily as a vitality tonic, especially during seasonal transitions or chronic fatigue.

Four-Guard Herbal Defense *(Inspired by Traditional Four Thieves Blend)*

Ingredients:

- 1 tsp Sage
- ½ tsp Thyme
- ½ tsp Rosemary
- ½ tsp Peppermint

Instructions

Steep all herbs together in hot water for 10–15 minutes. Cover to retain essential oils. Strain and drink warm.

Precautions:

- Avoid sage and rosemary in high doses during pregnancy.
- Thyme may stimulate menstruation in sensitive individuals.

Dosage/Use:

Drink 1 cup daily or at the first sign of illness for broad-spectrum support.

Cardiovascular Health

Promotes healthy blood flow, reduces tension, and nourishes the heart.

Heart & Circulation Support Tea

Ingredients:

- 1 part hawthorn berry
- 1 part linden flower
- 1 part hibiscus
- 1/2 part cinnamon chips

Instructions

Mix herbs thoroughly. Simmer 1 tablespoon in 2 cups water for 15–20 minutes. Strain and drink warm or cool.

Precautions:

- Consult with a physician if on heart or blood pressure medications.

Dosage/Use:

Drink 1–2 cups per day long-term for best benefits.

Summary: Key Takeaways

- Teas and infusions are simple, powerful, and versatile herbal tools.
- Learn to blend using **base + support + accent** herbs.
- Tailor teas for **digestion, rest, immunity, or energy** with specific plant allies.
- Infusions offer **more minerals and potency** than short steeps.
- Herbal tea rituals enhance both your health and your connection to nature.

Chapter 8

Syrups & Decoctions

Syrups and decoctions are foundational preparations in home apothecary. They are among the easiest and most enjoyable ways to extract and administer plant medicine—perfect for those new to herbalism. These methods use **water as a solvent** to extract medicinal compounds, making them safe, gentle, and suitable for most people, including children and the elderly.

Herbal syrups and decoctions have been used across cultures for centuries to manage **seasonal illnesses, respiratory issues, digestive discomfort**, and **immune challenges**. They require minimal tools—just **water, herbs, a pot**, and optional natural sweeteners like **honey** or **maple syrup**. Despite their simplicity, these preparations can be incredibly potent and therapeutic when made with intention and the right herbal combinations.

Immune Syrups & Respiratory Tonics

An **immune syrup** is a sweet, viscous herbal formula designed to **stimulate or modulate the immune system**. **Respiratory tonics** support lung function, soothe coughing, and ease congestion. Syrups are especially beneficial for children and picky adults who may resist taking tinctures.

Key Herbs for Syrups:

- **Elderberries** – Rich in antioxidants and antiviral compounds
- **Echinacea** – Stimulates immune response and helps fight infections
- **Mullein** – Expectorant and lung tonic
- **Marshmallow Root** – Demulcent that soothes mucous membranes
- **Thyme** – Antimicrobial and bronchodilator
- **Licorice Root** – Anti-inflammatory and harmonizing in formulas
- **Lemon Balm** – Calming, antiviral, and safe for most age groups

These herbs are simmered in water to extract their medicinal properties and then combined with a sweetener like **raw honey** or **vegetable glycerin**. Honey not only preserves the formula but also offers its own **antibacterial** and **soothing** properties.

Best Used:

- At the **first sign of illness**
- For **daily immune support** during cold/flu season
- As a **lung tonic** to help with allergies, bronchitis, or dry coughs

Root & Bark-Based Decoctions

Unlike syrups, which often use **flowers or leaves**, **decoctions** are meant for **tougher plant parts** like **roots**, **bark**, or **seeds**. These parts contain potent medicinal compounds that require **longer, sustained simmering** to extract.

Herbs Best Suited for Decoction:

- **Dandelion Root** – Detoxifying and liver-supportive
- **Burdock Root** – Blood purifier and skin tonic
- **Ginger Root** – Warming, anti-nausea, circulatory stimulant
- **Licorice Root** – Adaptogenic and demulcent
- **Cinnamon Bark** – Antimicrobial, digestive, and blood sugar support
- **Slippery Elm Bark** – Soothes irritated tissues in the gut and throat

How to Make a Basic Decoction:

1. Use **1 tablespoon** dried root/bark per **1 cup of water**
2. Add herbs and water to a pot (non-aluminum)
3. Bring to a boil, then reduce heat
4. **Simmer for 20–45 minutes** (covered to reduce evaporation)
5. Strain, cool slightly, and serve warm or chilled

Many decoctions can be turned into syrups by adding **honey or maple syrup** after straining and cooling.

Best Used For:

- Supporting **digestion, detoxification**, and **elimination pathways**
- Chronic conditions requiring **deep nourishment**
- Internal **tissue healing** (e.g., respiratory mucosa, digestive tract)

32 Syrup & Decoction Formulas

Herbal Syrup Formulas

Elderberry Immune Boost Syrup

Function: Stimulates immune defense and helps prevent viral infections.

Ingredients:

- 1 cup dried elderberries
- 2 tablespoons dried ginger root
- 1 cinnamon stick
- 4 cups water
- 1 cup raw honey

Instructions:

1. Add elderberries, ginger, and cinnamon to a pot with water.
2. Bring to a boil, then reduce heat and simmer for about 40 minutes, until liquid is reduced by half.
3. Strain through a fine mesh or cheesecloth into a clean bowl.
4. Let it cool slightly, then stir in the honey until well mixed.
5. Pour into a sterilized glass jar and store in the refrigerator.

Dosage:

- Adults: 1 tablespoon daily for prevention, or every 3 hours when ill.
- Children (over 2 years): 1 teaspoon.

Precautions:

- Do not give to children under 1 year due to honey content.
- Discontinue use if allergic reactions occur.

Marshmallow & Thyme Cough Syrup

Function: Soothes dry, spasmodic coughs and supports irritated throat tissues.

Ingredients:

- 1/2 cup dried marshmallow root
- 1/4 cup dried thyme leaves
- 3 cups water
- 3/4 cup raw honey

Instructions:

1. Combine herbs and water in a pot and bring to a gentle simmer.
2. Simmer uncovered for about 30 minutes.
3. Strain the herbs using cheesecloth or a fine mesh strainer.

4. Allow the liquid to cool slightly, then stir in the honey.
5. Store in a dark glass jar or bottle in the refrigerator for up to 2 months.

Dosage:

- Adults: 1 teaspoon to 1 tablespoon, up to 4 times per day as needed.
- Children: 1/2 teaspoon as needed.

Precautions:

- Be sure to strain thoroughly; marshmallow root is mucilaginous and can clog strainers.
- Space at least 2 hours from medications, as marshmallow may delay their absorption.

Lemon Balm & Elderflower Fever Syrup

Function: Reduces mild fevers, especially in children. Calming, cooling, and antiviral.

Ingredients:

- 1/2 cup dried lemon balm
- 1/4 cup dried elderflowers
- 2 cups water
- 1/2 cup honey

Instructions:

1. Combine herbs and water in a saucepan.
2. Simmer on low for 20–25 minutes.
3. Strain, let cool slightly, and stir in honey.
4. Bottle and refrigerate for up to 2 months.

Dosage:

- 1 tsp every 2–3 hours during fever.
- Safe for children over 2.

Precautions:

Avoid in hypothyroidism (lemon balm may suppress thyroid in high doses).

Ginger & Fennel Digestive Aid Syrup

Function: Eases bloating, gas, and sluggish digestion.

Ingredients:

- 2 tbsp dried ginger root
- 1 tbsp fennel seeds
- 2.5 cups water
- 3/4 cup honey

Instructions:

1. Simmer herbs in water for 30 minutes.
2. Strain and combine with honey.
3. Store in a cool, dark place or refrigerate.

Dosage:

1 tsp after meals.

Precautions:

Avoid with ulcers or sensitive stomachs (ginger may irritate in high doses).

Calendula Skin Support Syrup

Function: Supports lymph flow and skin detoxification.

Ingredients:

- 1/2 cup dried calendula flowers
- 1 tbsp cleavers
- 3 cups water
- 3/4 cup honey

Instructions:

Same process: simmer, strain, mix in honey, store.

Dosage:

1 tbsp daily.

Precautions:

Avoid if allergic to ragweed family.

Holy Basil (Tulsi) Stress Syrup

Function: Adaptogen; calms nerves and supports adrenal health.

Ingredients:

- 1/2 cup dried tulsi
- 1/4 cup dried lemon balm
- 3 cups water
- 3/4 cup honey

Instructions:

Simmer for 25 minutes, strain, cool, add honey.

Dosage:

1 tbsp 1–2x/day.

Precautions:

Avoid during pregnancy unless directed by a practitioner.

Lavender & Skullcap Sleep Syrup

Function: Supports deeper, restful sleep.

Ingredients:

- 1/4 cup lavender flowers
- 1/2 cup skullcap
- 2.5 cups water
- 1/2 cup honey

Instructions:

Simmer gently, strain, add honey, refrigerate.

Dosage:

1 tbsp before bed.

Precautions:

May cause drowsiness.

Elderberry & Nettle Iron Syrup

Function: Replenishes iron, supports fatigue and anemia.

Ingredients:

- 1/2 cup dried elderberries
- 1/2 cup dried nettle leaf
- 3 cups water
- 3/4 cup blackstrap molasses (iron-rich)

Instructions:

Simmer herbs in water, strain, add molasses.

Dosage:

1 tbsp daily with food.

Precautions:

Consult your doctor if you're on iron supplements.

Garlic & Thyme Cold Syrup

Function: Antimicrobial and decongestant.

Ingredients:

- 3–4 cloves crushed garlic
- 1 tbsp dried thyme
- 1 lemon (sliced)
- 1/2 cup raw honey

Instructions:

Layer garlic, thyme, and lemon in a jar; pour honey to cover. Let sit 24–48 hrs before use.

Dosage:

1 tsp every 2–3 hours.

Precautions:

Avoid on empty stomach; garlic can cause nausea.

Peppermint & Catnip Cooling Fever Syrup

Function: Helps reduce heat during fevers and calms restlessness.

Ingredients:

- 1/2 cup peppermint
- 1/2 cup catnip
- 3 cups water
- 3/4 cup honey

Dosage:

1 tsp every few hours as needed.

Precautions:

Peppermint may irritate those with acid reflux.

Plantain & Licorice Sore Throat Syrup

Function: Coats and soothes irritated mucous membranes.

Ingredients:

- 1/4 cup dried plantain leaf
- 1 tbsp licorice root
- 3 cups water
- 3/4 cup honey

Dosage:

1 tsp every 2–3 hours.

Precautions:

Licorice may raise blood pressure with long-term use.

Passionflower & Blue Vervain Nerve Syrup

Function: Eases tension, supports nervous system recovery.

Ingredients:

- 1/4 cup each of passionflower and blue vervain
- 2.5 cups water
- 3/4 cup honey

Dosage:

1 tbsp morning and night.

Precautions:

Use with caution if on sedatives or antidepressants.

Red Clover & Chickweed Skin Cleansing Syrup

Function: Gently detoxifies and supports skin conditions.

Ingredients:

- 1/4 cup red clover
- 1/4 cup chickweed
- 3 cups water
- 1/2 cup honey

Dosage:

1 tbsp daily for 2–3 weeks.

Precautions:

Avoid red clover during pregnancy or with estrogen-sensitive conditions.

Ashwagandha & Cinnamon Adrenal Syrup

Function: Rebuilds energy and combats fatigue.

Ingredients:

- 1/2 cup ashwagandha root
- 1 cinnamon stick
- 3.5 cups water
- 3/4 cup honey

Dosage:

1 tbsp daily in the morning.

Precautions:

Avoid during pregnancy; may be too stimulating for some at night.

Hibiscus & Lemon Cooling Heart Tonic Syrup

Function: Lowers blood pressure and supports circulation.

Ingredients:

- 1/2 cup dried hibiscus petals
- 1 lemon (sliced)
- 3 cups water
- 3/4 cup honey

Dosage:

1 tbsp daily, chilled or over ice.

Precautions:

May interact with blood pressure meds—monitor carefully.

Herbal Decoction Formulas

Dandelion Detox Decoction

Function: Supports liver function and gentle detoxification.

Ingredients:

- 1 tbsp dried dandelion root
- 1 tbsp dried burdock root
- 3 cups water

Instructions:

1. Combine roots and water in a saucepan.
2. Simmer gently for 30–40 minutes.
3. Strain and drink 1 cup warm.

Dosage:

1 cup, 1–2x/day for 7–10 days.

Precautions:

Avoid if allergic to ragweed family.

Ginger-Cinnamon Circulatory Tonic

Function: Warms the body, promotes circulation, and improves digestion.

Ingredients:

- 1 tbsp fresh or dried ginger root
- 1 stick cinnamon
- 2.5 cups water

Instructions:

Simmer for 25 minutes. Strain and sip warm.

Dosage:

1 cup in the morning or before cold exposure.

Precautions:

Avoid in acute inflammation or fever.

Burdock & Licorice Skin Cleanse Decoction

Function: Supports skin, blood, and lymphatic cleansing.

Ingredients:

- 1 tbsp burdock root
- 1 tsp licorice root
- 3 cups water

Instructions:

Simmer for 30 minutes. Strain.

Dosage:

1 cup daily for 2 weeks.

Precautions:

Avoid licorice with high blood pressure.

Ashwagandha Stress Relief Decoction

Function: Adaptogen for adrenal support and nervous system nourishment.

Ingredients:

- 1 tbsp dried ashwagandha root
- 3 cups water

Instructions:

Simmer gently for 30 minutes. Strain and drink before bed.

Dosage:

1 cup nightly or 1–2x/day.

Precautions:

Consult with doctor if on thyroid meds.

Milk Thistle Liver Support Decoction

Function: Helps regenerate and protect liver cells.

Ingredients:

- 1 tbsp crushed milk thistle seeds
- 3 cups water

Instructions:

Simmer for 20 minutes, then steep covered for 10 more. Strain.

Dosage:

1 cup daily.

Precautions:

Avoid in allergy to daisies/ragweed.

Valerian Root Sleep Support Decoction

Function: Promotes deep sleep and nervous system relaxation.

Ingredients:

- 1 tbsp dried valerian root
- 2 cups water

Instructions:

Simmer 15–20 minutes. Strain and drink 30 minutes before bed.

Dosage:

1/2 to 1 cup before sleep.

Precautions:

May cause vivid dreams or grogginess.

Slippery Elm Gut-Healing Decoction

Function: Soothes inflamed digestive tissues.

Ingredients:

- 1 tbsp slippery elm bark
- 3 cups water

Instructions:

Simmer for 20 minutes. Stir frequently. Strain.

Dosage:

1 cup 2x/day.

Precautions:

May slow absorption of medications. Separate by 2+ hours.

Cinnamon & Fennel Digestive Decoction

Function: Eases bloating, gas, and sluggish digestion.

Ingredients:

- 1 stick cinnamon
- 1 tsp fennel seeds
- 2.5 cups water

Instructions:

Simmer for 25 minutes. Strain.

Dosage:

1/2–1 cup before or after meals.

Precautions:

Safe short term. Avoid during pregnancy in high doses.

Blue Vervain Nervous System Tonic

Function: Supports emotional balance and tension relief.

Ingredients:

- 1 tbsp dried blue vervain
- 2 cups water

Instructions:

Simmer for 20 minutes. Strain and sip.

Dosage:

1/2 cup up to 2x/day.

Precautions:

Bitter taste. May lower blood pressure.

Goldenseal Antimicrobial Decoction

Function: Natural antibacterial, antifungal, and antiviral.

Ingredients:

- 1 tsp goldenseal root
- 2 cups water

Instructions:

Simmer for 20–25 minutes. Strain.

Dosage:

1/4 cup 2x/day for short-term infections.

Precautions:

Not for long-term use or pregnancy.

Garlic & Ginger Infection Fighter Decoction

Function: Combats infection, boosts immunity, clears congestion.

Ingredients:

- 2 cloves crushed garlic
- 1 tbsp fresh ginger
- 3 cups water

Instructions:

Simmer for 20 minutes. Strain and sip warm.

Dosage:

1 cup 2x/day during illness.

Precautions:

Avoid raw garlic on empty stomach.

Comfrey Bone & Tissue Repair Decoction

Function: Traditionally used to support bone healing ("knit bone").

Ingredients:

- 1 tbsp dried comfrey root
- 3 cups water

Instructions:

Simmer gently for 30 minutes. Strain.

Dosage:

1/4–1/2 cup daily for short-term internal use only.

Precautions:

Internal use should be brief; consult qualified herbalist.

Oatstraw Nervous System Nourishment Decoction

Function: Mineral-rich tonic for burnout and stress recovery.

Ingredients:

- 1 tbsp dried oatstraw
- 3 cups water

Instructions:

Simmer for 30–40 minutes. Strain.

Dosage:

1 cup 1–2x/day.

Precautions:

Safe for daily use unless gluten-sensitive.

Horsetail Silica Support Decoction

Function: Strengthens hair, nails, and connective tissues.

Ingredients:

- 1 tbsp dried horsetail
- 2.5 cups water

Instructions:

Simmer for 20 minutes. Strain and drink warm.

Dosage:

1/2 cup daily.

Precautions:

Use short-term only; may irritate kidneys if overused.

Red Clover Detox & Hormone Balance Decoction

Function: Gently supports hormonal health and blood purification.

Ingredients:

- 1 tbsp dried red clover blossoms
- 3 cups water

Instructions:

Simmer for 25 minutes. Strain.

Dosage:

1 cup daily or every other day.

Precautions:

Avoid during pregnancy or if taking blood thinners.

Ginger & Cinnamon Digestive Warming Decoction

Function: Enhances digestion, circulation, and reduces nausea.

Ingredients:

- 1 tbsp sliced fresh or dried ginger
- 1 cinnamon stick
- 3 cups water

Instructions:

Simmer for 25 minutes, strain. Sweeten lightly if desired.

Dosage:

1 cup after meals.

Precautions:

Avoid in pregnancy or bleeding disorders in large doses

Licorice & Marshmallow Gut Soother Decoction

Function: Soothes gut lining and supports digestion.

Ingredients:

- 1 tbsp licorice root
- 1 tbsp marshmallow root
- 3 cups water

Instructions:

Simmer for 30 minutes. Strain and drink warm.

Dosage:

1 cup 2x per day.

Precautions:

Licorice may elevate blood pressure; limit long-term use.

Chapter 9

Tinctures & Liquid Extracts

What Are Tinctures and Why Are They So Powerful?

Tinctures are one of the most **concentrated**, **convenient**, and **long-lasting** ways to preserve the medicinal power of herbs. At their core, tinctures are **liquid extracts** made by soaking plant material in a solvent that pulls out its active constituents.

Unlike teas, which are water-based and spoil quickly, tinctures can last for **years**. You only need a few drops at a time to receive the same effect as cups of tea.

They are:

- Easy to carry and dose (great for travel or emergencies)
- Highly concentrated (just 20–30 drops = a therapeutic dose)
- Fast-acting (especially under the tongue)
- Shelf-stable for years if stored properly

Whether you're treating a cold, calming anxiety, easing pain, or supporting digestion, tinctures allow you to **customize herbal care in seconds**.

Solvent, Strength & Storage

The **solvent** (also called the menstruum) you choose will determine:

- What types of herbal compounds you extract (e.g., alkaloids, tannins, resins, aromatics)
- The shelf-life and potency
- Who it's suitable for (children, adults, pets, pregnant women, etc.)

The three most common tincture solvents are:

1. **Alcohol-Based Tinctures** (Traditional Tinctures)

What They Are:

Herbs soaked in a strong alcohol (typically vodka, brandy, or grain alcohol). Alcohol is the most powerful and broad-spectrum solvent available.

What They Extract:

✓ Alkaloids
✓ Resins
✓ Essential oils
✓ Flavonoids
✓ Tannins
✓ Bitters

Shelf Life: 5+ years (longest of all solvents)

Who It's For:

- Adults and teens
- Not recommended for young children or recovering alcoholics (unless under professional guidance)

How To Make:

1. **Chop** the herb (fresh or dried) finely to increase surface area.
2. **Fill** a clean glass jar ½ to ¾ full with herbs.
3. **Cover completely** with alcohol (vodka or brandy 40–60% is ideal).
4. **Seal tightly**, label (name, date, ratio, alcohol type), and store in a cool, dark place.
5. **Shake daily** for 4–6 weeks.
6. **Strain** through cheesecloth, pressing well to extract all liquid.
7. **Bottle** in amber dropper bottles and label clearly.

💡 Example:

- *Echinacea Root Tincture*: 1:5 dried root to 60% alcohol. Use at the first sign of illness.

2. **Vinegar-Based Extracts** (Acetates)

What They Are:

Herbs extracted in raw, unfiltered **apple cider vinegar** (ACV). Vinegar has been used for centuries as a natural medicine and food preservative.

What They Extract:

✓ Alkaloids
✓ Some minerals
✓ Water-soluble vitamins
✓ Mild acids

Flavor: Tangy and strong—can be diluted in juice or honey

Shelf Life: 6 months to 1 year

Who It's For:

- Kids and sensitive individuals
- Great alternative when alcohol is inappropriate
- Ideal for culinary remedies (like **fire cider**, an immune-boosting vinegar infusion)

How To Make:

Same steps as alcohol tincture—just substitute alcohol with raw apple cider vinegar.
Use **plastic or wax-lined metal lids**, as vinegar corrodes metal.

Tip: Vinegar extracts are excellent for extracting calcium and magnesium from mineral-rich herbs like **nettles** and **red raspberry leaf**.

3. **Glycerin-Based Extracts** (Glycerites)

What They Are:

Sweet, syrup-like tinctures made using **vegetable glycerin**, a clear, non-alcoholic liquid derived from fats.

What They Extract:

✓ Sugars
✓ Glycosides
✓ Some alkaloids
✓ Water-soluble compounds

Shelf Life: 1–2 years

Who It's For:

- Children, pets, and sensitive adults

- Ideal for people avoiding alcohol entirely
- Sweet tasting—easy for kids to take

How To Make:

1. Use **60% glycerin / 40% distilled water** as your solvent mix.
2. Combine with your chopped herb in a jar (just like other tinctures).
3. Steep for 4–6 weeks, shaking daily.
4. Strain and store in a dropper bottle.

Tip: Glycerites are perfect for herbs like **lemon balm**, **licorice**, or **chamomile**—gentle, calming, and sweet.

Herbal Ratios & Dosage Guidelines

Herb Form	Typical Ratio (Herb:Solvent)
Fresh Herb	1:2 (1 part herb to 2 parts solvent)
Dried Herb	1:5 (1 part herb to 5 parts solvent)

Dosage Guidelines (Adults):

- Standard: 20–40 drops (about 1 dropperful) in water, 2–3x daily
- Acute Issues: Up to every 2 hours, based on safety of herb

Always **label your tincture** with:

- Herb name (common + Latin)
- Solvent used + strength
- Date made and strained
- Dosage and purpose (optional)

Custom Herbal Tincture By Ailment

These formulas are excellent starting points. You can use **individual herbs** or make **synergistic blends** by combining 2–4 herbs per formula. A more detailed recipe is given in the later part of this chapter.

Anxiety & Stress Relief Formula

Function: Calms the nervous system, reduces tension, and improves resilience to stress.

Formula:

- 1 part Passionflower
- 1 part Lemon Balm
- 1 part Holy Basil (Tulsi)
- ½ part Skullcap

Instructions:

1. Blend dried herbs and place in a jar.
2. Add 40–60% alcohol to cover herbs (1:5 ratio).
3. Label and steep for 4–6 weeks, shaking daily.
4. Strain and store in amber dropper bottles.

Adult Dosage: 30 drops up to 3 times daily during stress.
Child Dosage: 10–12 drops diluted in water (age 7+).

Precautions:

- Avoid in hypothyroidism (lemon balm).
- May increase sedation with other calming agents.

Sleep Support Formula

Function: Promotes restful sleep, reduces racing thoughts, and improves sleep onset.

Formula:

- 1 part Valerian
- 1 part Passionflower
- 1 part Hops
- ½ part Chamomile

Instructions:

1. Combine herbs in a jar with 60% alcohol (1:5 ratio).
2. Seal, label, and shake daily for 6 weeks.
3. Strain and store in amber bottles.

Adult Dosage: 30–40 drops 30 minutes before bedtime.
Child Dosage: 10–15 drops diluted in warm tea (age 8+).

Precautions:

- May cause morning grogginess (valerian).
- Avoid combining with other sleep medications.

Digestive Ease Formula

Function: Eases bloating, gas, nausea, indigestion, and stimulates bile and enzymes.

Formula:

- 1 part Peppermint
- 1 part Fennel
- 1 part Ginger
- ½ part Dandelion Root

Instructions:

1. Combine herbs and steep in 60% alcohol for 4 weeks.
2. Shake daily, strain, and bottle.

Adult Dosage: 30 drops before or after meals.
Child Dosage: 8–10 drops in warm water or tea.

Precautions:

- Avoid peppermint in reflux sufferers.
- Dandelion may increase bile flow—avoid with gallstones.

Cold & Flu Acute Formula

Function: Antiviral, fever-reducing, and immune-supportive during acute infection.

Formula:

- 1 part Elderberry
- 1 part Echinacea
- 1 part Yarrow

- ½ part Thyme

Instructions:

1. Combine herbs and add 40% alcohol.
2. Shake daily for 4–6 weeks, strain and store.

Adult Dosage: 30 drops every 2–3 hours during infection.
Child Dosage: 10–12 drops in tea (age 5+).

Precautions:

- Not for autoimmune conditions (echinacea).
- Do not use raw elderberries (must be pre-cooked if fresh).

Immune Support & Prevention Formula

Function: Strengthens immune resilience and prevents frequent infections.

Formula:

- 1 part Holy Basil (Tulsi)
- 1 part Astragalus (optional addition, if available)
- 1 part Elderberry
- ½ part Licorice Root

Instructions:

1. Place herbs in a jar, cover with 40–60% alcohol or glycerin.
2. Steep 4–6 weeks, shaking daily.
3. Strain and pour into dropper bottles.

Adult Dosage: 30 drops once or twice daily during flu season.
Child Dosage: 10–12 drops daily in warm water (age 6+).

Precautions:

- Licorice not for long-term use in hypertension.
- Holy basil may lower blood sugar.

Hormonal Balance & PMS Relief Formula

Function: Regulates female hormonal cycles, reduces PMS symptoms, and tones the uterus.

Formula:

- 1 part Red Raspberry Leaf
- 1 part Licorice Root
- 1 part Lemon Balm
- ½ part Chamomile

Instructions:

1. Blend herbs and place in a sterilized jar.
2. Add 40% vodka or apple cider vinegar to cover (1:5 ratio).
3. Label, shake daily for 4–6 weeks.
4. Strain and pour into dropper bottles.

Adult Dosage: 30 drops 2 times daily starting mid-cycle to menstruation.
Child Dosage: 10–12 drops for teens with menstrual cramps.

Precautions:

- Avoid licorice in hypertension.
- Raspberry leaf should be used cautiously early in pregnancy.

Liver Detox & Support Formula

Function: Stimulates detoxification, supports bile flow, and regenerates liver tissue.

Formula:

- 1 part Dandelion Root
- 1 part Burdock Root
- 1 part Milk Thistle Seed (crushed)
- ½ part Ginger Root

Instructions:

1. Place herbs in a glass jar and cover with 60% alcohol.
2. Label, shake daily for 6 weeks.
3. Strain and store in amber dropper bottles.

Adult Dosage: 30 drops before meals or 2x daily for 3–4 weeks.
Child Dosage: 10 drops diluted in tea (age 6+).

Precautions:

- Monitor liver medications with milk thistle.
- Dandelion may be contraindicated with gallstones.

Respiratory Support Formula

Function: Supports expectoration, soothes coughs, and strengthens lung tissues.

Formula:

- 1 part Mullein
- 1 part Thyme
- 1 part Elecampane
- ½ part Licorice Root

Instructions:

1. Mix herbs and cover with 60% alcohol or glycerin.
2. Steep 4–6 weeks, shaking regularly.
3. Strain and store.

Adult Dosage: 30 drops every 3–4 hours for cough or congestion.
Child Dosage: 10–12 drops in warm tea (age 6+).

Precautions:

- Elecampane is strong—short-term use only.
- Filter mullein tincture well to avoid irritation.

Menstrual Cramps & Pain Relief Formula

Function: Relieves uterine tension, reduces pain, and promotes emotional calm during menstruation.

Formula:

- 1 part Chamomile

- 1 part Passionflower
- 1 part Skullcap
- ½ part Red Raspberry Leaf

Instructions:

1. Blend and add to jar with 40% vodka.
2. Shake daily and steep for 4 weeks.
3. Strain and pour into dropper bottles.

Adult Dosage: 30 drops every 4 hours during cramping.
Child Dosage: 10–12 drops in warm water (for teens).

Precautions:

- Avoid passionflower during early pregnancy.
- Skullcap enhances sedation; don't combine with sleep meds.

Cognitive Focus & Memory Formula

Function: Enhances memory, focus, and circulation to the brain.

Formula:

- 1 part Rosemary
- 1 part Holy Basil (Tulsi)
- ½ part Peppermint
- ½ part Nettle

Instructions:

1. Combine herbs and cover with 40% alcohol.
2. Shake daily and steep for 4–6 weeks.
3. Strain and bottle.

Adult Dosage: 30 drops in the morning and afternoon.
Child Dosage: 10–12 drops (age 8+) in tea or juice.

Precautions:

- Rosemary may overstimulate before bed.
- Monitor blood sugar if taking tulsi long term.

Skin Conditions & Detox Formula

Function: Supports skin health by purifying blood and enhancing detox pathways.

Formula:

- 1 part Burdock Root
- 1 part Nettle Leaf
- 1 part Dandelion Root
- ½ part Calendula Flowers

Instructions:

1. Combine herbs and add to a jar.
2. Cover with 60% alcohol (1:5 herb-to-liquid ratio).
3. Label, shake daily for 6 weeks.
4. Strain and bottle in amber dropper jars.

Adult Dosage: 30 drops twice daily for skin issues (acne, eczema, psoriasis).
Child Dosage: 10–12 drops in juice or warm water (age 6+).

Precautions:

- Burdock is diuretic—drink plenty of water.
- Calendula should be used cautiously internally during pregnancy.

Allergy Relief Formula

Function: Reduces seasonal allergies, nasal inflammation, and immune overreaction.

Formula:

- 1 part Nettle Leaf
- 1 part Lemon Balm
- 1 part Licorice Root
- ½ part Chamomile

Instructions:

1. Blend herbs and cover with 40% vodka or glycerin.
2. Shake daily and let sit for 4–6 weeks.
3. Strain and store in amber bottles.

Adult Dosage: 30 drops up to 3 times daily during allergy season.
Child Dosage: 10–15 drops in warm tea or water.

Precautions:

- Licorice should not be used long-term with high blood pressure.
- Lemon balm may interfere with thyroid function in sensitive individuals.

Kidney & Urinary Tract Support Formula

Function: Promotes healthy urination, reduces water retention, and supports urinary tract health.

Formula:

- 1 part Nettle Leaf
- 1 part Dandelion Leaf (or Root)
- 1 part Marshmallow Root
- ½ part Calendula Flowers

Instructions:

1. Mix herbs and soak in 40–50% alcohol or glycerin.
2. Shake daily for 4–6 weeks.
3. Strain and pour into dropper bottles.

Adult Dosage: 30 drops 2–3 times daily.
Child Dosage: 10 drops in herbal tea (age 5+).

Precautions:

- May increase urination—maintain hydration.
- Avoid dandelion leaf in potassium-sparing therapy.

Heart & Circulation Support Formula

Function: Strengthens the heart, regulates blood pressure, and supports circulation.

Formula:

- 1 part Hawthorn Berries

- 1 part Rosemary
- ½ part Ginger
- ½ part Holy Basil (Tulsi)

Instructions:

1. Place herbs in a clean jar and cover with 40–50% alcohol.
2. Shake daily and steep for 4–6 weeks.
3. Strain and bottle in dark glass.

Adult Dosage: 30–40 drops twice daily for at least 3 months.
Child Dosage: 10–12 drops in warm tea (age 10+).

Precautions:

- Hawthorn may potentiate heart medications—consult if on blood pressure drugs.
- Avoid rosemary with seizure disorders.

Adrenal Fatigue & Energy Support Formula

Function: Restores depleted energy, balances stress hormones, and supports adrenal function.

Formula:

- 1 part Ashwagandha Root
- 1 part Licorice Root
- 1 part Holy Basil (Tulsi)
- ½ part Nettle Leaf

Instructions:

1. Combine herbs in a glass jar and add 60% alcohol.
2. Label, shake daily for 6 weeks.
3. Strain and store in amber dropper bottles.

Adult Dosage: 30 drops in morning and afternoon (avoid late evening).
Child Dosage: Generally not recommended under age 12 without guidance.

Precautions:

- Avoid long-term licorice use in those with high blood pressure.
- Ashwagandha may not be suitable for hyperthyroid individuals

Bottling, Storage & Shelf Life Tips

Best Practices:

- Use **amber or cobalt blue glass bottles** to protect from light
- Store in a **cool, dry, dark** cabinet
- Avoid contamination by keeping droppers clean
- Label each tincture clearly

Solvent	Shelf Life
Alcohol	5+ years
Vinegar	~1 year
Glycerin	1–2 years

Common Beginner Questions:

Can I use vodka from the store?

Yes! Use 80–100 proof vodka (40–50% alcohol) for most tinctures. Higher-proof alcohol (like Everclear) is used for fresh herbs or resinous plants.

Can I mix herbs together?

Absolutely. Many formulas are **blends**. Just make sure the herbs support the same purpose and are safe in combination.

How do I know it's done extracting?

After 4–6 weeks, your tincture will appear darker and richer. The scent should be strong and true to the herb.

Quick Tincture Kit (Starter Supplies)

- Glass jars with lids (mason jars work well)
- Amber glass dropper bottles (1 oz or 2 oz)
- Fine mesh strainer or cheesecloth
- Funnel
- Labels + pen

- High-proof alcohol / ACV / vegetable glycerin

---

30 Tincture Remedies

Chamomile Calm Tincture

Function: Promotes relaxation, eases anxiety, supports digestion, and aids sleep.

Ingredients:

- 1 cup dried chamomile flowers
- 2.5 cups 40% alcohol (vodka or brandy)

Instructions:

1. Place chamomile flowers into a clean glass jar.
2. Pour alcohol over the herbs until completely submerged.
3. Seal tightly, label with date and contents.
4. Shake daily and store in a cool, dark space for 4–6 weeks.
5. Strain through cheesecloth or a fine strainer.
6. Transfer to amber glass dropper bottles.

Adult Dosage: 30 drops in a small glass of water or tea, 2–3 times daily or at bedtime.

Child Dosage: 10–15 drops diluted in warm water or tea before bed.

Precautions:

- May cause allergic reactions in those with ragweed or aster family sensitivities.
- Use cautiously during pregnancy and avoid excessive dosing.

Lavender Nerve-Soothing Tincture

Function: Soothes nervous tension, reduces irritability, and supports restful sleep.

Ingredients:

- 1 cup dried lavender buds
- 2.5 cups 40% vodka

Instructions:

1. Add lavender buds to a jar and cover with alcohol.
2. Label and store in a dark place for 4–6 weeks, shaking daily.
3. Strain and transfer to amber bottles.

Adult Dosage: 20–30 drops in water, up to 3 times daily.

Child Dosage: 5–10 drops diluted in water or tea.

Precautions:

- Avoid in early pregnancy in high doses.
- May cause drowsiness.

Peppermint Digestive Ease Tincture

Function: Relieves bloating, gas, and indigestion; stimulates appetite.

Ingredients:

- 1 cup dried peppermint leaves
- 2.5 cups 40% vodka

Instructions:

1. Fill jar with peppermint leaves and cover with vodka.
2. Label and let sit 4–6 weeks, shaking daily.
3. Strain and bottle in dark glass jars.

Adult Dosage: 30 drops before or after meals.

Child Dosage: 5–10 drops diluted in warm water.

Precautions:

- May worsen acid reflux.
- Avoid use during pregnancy if unsure of safety.

Lemon Balm Uplift Tincture

Function: Mild antidepressant, antiviral, calms anxiety, and supports restful sleep.

Ingredients:

- 1 cup dried lemon balm leaves
- 2.5 cups 60% vegetable glycerin + 40% distilled water (for alcohol-free version)

Instructions:

1. Place lemon balm and glycerin mixture in a clean glass jar.
2. Seal, label, and store in a cool, dark location for 4–6 weeks.
3. Shake daily to ensure thorough extraction.
4. After steeping, strain through cheesecloth or fine mesh.
5. Pour into amber dropper bottles for use.

Adult Dosage: 30–40 drops up to 3 times daily.

Child Dosage: 10–15 drops in tea or juice.

Precautions:

- May interfere with thyroid medications.
- Avoid high doses in individuals with hypothyroidism.

Ginger Root Digestive Tonic

Function: Stimulates digestion, improves circulation, relieves nausea and cramps.

Ingredients:

- 1 cup fresh grated ginger root
- 2 cups 95% alcohol (e.g. Everclear)

Instructions:

1. Place fresh ginger into a clean jar.
2. Pour alcohol over the root to cover completely.
3. Seal, label, and shake daily for 4 weeks.
4. Strain using cheesecloth and bottle in amber dropper bottles.

Adult Dosage: 20 drops before meals or during nausea.

Child Dosage: 5–8 drops in honey water or tea.

Precautions:

- May interact with blood thinners.
- Large doses in pregnancy should be avoided unless supervised.

Echinacea Immune Defense Tincture

Function: Boosts immune response; useful at the onset of colds, flu, or infections.

Ingredients:

- 1 cup dried echinacea root
- 2.5 cups 60% alcohol

Instructions:

1. Place echinacea root in a glass jar and cover with alcohol.
2. Seal and label the jar, store in a cool, dark place for 4–6 weeks.
3. Shake daily to promote full extraction.
4. Strain through cheesecloth and pour into dropper bottles.

Adult Dosage: 30 drops every 2 hours at first sign of illness (max 5x/day).

Child Dosage: 10–15 drops in water, 3x/day during illness.

Precautions:

- Not for long-term use (limit to 10–14 days).
- Avoid in autoimmune conditions unless directed by a professional.

Elderberry Flu-Fighter Tincture

Function: Antiviral and antioxidant-rich; supports the immune system and shortens flu duration.

Ingredients:

- 1 cup dried elderberries
- 2.5 cups 40% alcohol or 60% glycerin

Instructions:

1. Simmer elderberries in a bit of water for 15 minutes to deactivate compounds.
2. Cool, then place in jar and add alcohol or glycerin.
3. Label and shake daily for 4–6 weeks.
4. Strain through cloth and bottle for use.

Adult Dosage: 30 drops every 3 hours at onset of cold or flu.

Child Dosage: 10–12 drops in juice or warm water, up to 4x/day.

Precautions:

- Never use raw elderberries.
- For children under 2, consult a healthcare provider.

Ashwagandha Adrenal Rebuilder

Function: Adaptogen; balances stress hormones, supports energy, promotes restful sleep.

Ingredients:

- 1 cup dried ashwagandha root
- 2.5 cups 60% alcohol

Instructions:

1. Add ashwagandha root to a jar and cover with alcohol.
2. Seal, label, and shake daily for 4–6 weeks.
3. Strain and store in amber glass dropper bottles.

Adult Dosage: 30 drops at night or in the morning for 4–6 weeks.

Child Dosage: Not recommended for children under 12 unless advised.

Precautions:

- May interfere with thyroid or sedative medications.
- Avoid during pregnancy unless prescribed.

Holy Basil (Tulsi) Clarity Tincture

Function: Adaptogen; clears mental fog, balances mood, supports immune function.

Ingredients:

- 1 cup dried tulsi leaves
- 2.5 cups 40% alcohol or 60% glycerin

Instructions:

1. Place tulsi leaves in a glass jar and cover with solvent.
2. Label and store for 4–6 weeks, shaking daily.
3. Strain and store in dark dropper bottles.

Adult Dosage: 25–30 drops 1–2 times daily.

Child Dosage: 5–10 drops diluted in tea or juice.

Precautions:

- May lower blood sugar.
- Use with caution in hypoglycemia.

Skullcap Nervous System Tincture

Function: Eases nervous tension, racing thoughts, and supports sleep in times of stress.

Ingredients:

- 1 cup dried skullcap (aerial parts)
- 2.5 cups 40% vodka

Instructions:

1. Fill a clean jar with skullcap and pour alcohol to cover.
2. Seal and label, store in a dark space for 6 weeks.
3. Shake daily, strain, and transfer to dropper bottles.

Adult Dosage: 30 drops at bedtime or during acute stress.

Child Dosage: 10–12 drops diluted in tea before sleep.

Precautions:

- Use with caution when taking other sedatives.
- Do not exceed recommended dosage.

Valerian Sleep Support Tincture

Function: Deeply sedative; relieves insomnia, anxiety, and promotes deep sleep.

Ingredients:

- 1 cup dried valerian root
- 2.5 cups 60% alcohol (vodka or brandy)

Instructions:

1. Place valerian root into a clean glass jar.
2. Pour alcohol over the herb until fully submerged.
3. Seal tightly, label with date and contents.
4. Store in a cool, dark place for 6 weeks, shaking daily.
5. Strain through cheesecloth and bottle in amber glass jars.

Adult Dosage: 30–40 drops 30 minutes before bed.

Child Dosage: 10–12 drops (age 8+), diluted in water or tea under professional guidance.

Precautions:

- May cause morning drowsiness.
- Avoid combining with alcohol or sedative drugs.

Passionflower Anxiety & Sleep Tincture

Function: Mild sedative; eases anxiety, racing thoughts, and supports restful sleep.

Ingredients:

- 1 cup dried passionflower
- 2.5 cups 40% vodka

Instructions:

1. Add passionflower to a clean jar and pour in alcohol.
2. Label and store for 4–6 weeks, shaking daily.
3. Strain and pour into dark dropper bottles.

Adult Dosage: 30 drops before bed or during anxiety episodes.

Child Dosage: 8–10 drops (age 7+), diluted in herbal tea.

Precautions:

- May enhance the effect of sedatives.
- Use cautiously in pregnancy.

Hops Rest & Digest Tincture

Function: Sleep-inducing, calming, and helps with digestive discomfort.

Ingredients:

- 1 cup dried hops
- 2.5 cups 40% vodka

Instructions:

1. Fill a jar with hops and pour alcohol to cover fully.
2. Label and shake daily for 4–6 weeks.
3. Strain and store in amber glass bottles.

Adult Dosage: 20–30 drops at bedtime or before meals.

Child Dosage: Not recommended for children under 12.

Precautions:

- May intensify symptoms of depression.
- May cause vivid dreams.

Calendula Skin & Lymph Tincture

Function: Anti-inflammatory, wound healing, and supports lymphatic movement.

Ingredients:

- 1 cup dried calendula flowers
- 2.5 cups 40% vodka or apple cider vinegar

Instructions:

1. Place calendula in a clean jar, add solvent to cover.
2. Shake daily for 4 weeks and keep in a cool, dark place.
3. Strain and bottle.

Adult Dosage: 20 drops twice daily for internal lymph support.

Child Dosage: 5–10 drops in water or juice.

Precautions:

- Internally avoid during pregnancy unless approved.
- Topical use is generally safe.

Yarrow Immune & Fever Tincture

Function: Reduces fever, promotes sweating, and supports immune health.

Ingredients:

- 1 cup dried yarrow leaves and flowers
- 2.5 cups 40% vodka

Instructions:

1. Fill a jar with yarrow and cover completely with alcohol.
2. Shake daily and store in a cool, dark location for 4–6 weeks.
3. Strain and transfer to dropper bottles.

Adult Dosage: 30 drops every 4 hours at onset of illness or fever.

Child Dosage: 10–15 drops diluted in warm water or tea.

Precautions:

- May cause allergic reactions in those sensitive to ragweed.
- Avoid during pregnancy.

Marshmallow Root Soothing Extract

Function: Soothes sore throat, dry cough, and inflamed mucous membranes.

Ingredients:

- 1 cup dried marshmallow root
- 2.5 cups 60% glycerin + 40% distilled water (alcohol-free)

Instructions:

1. Combine root and glycerin mixture in a glass jar.
2. Shake daily and store for 4–6 weeks.
3. Strain and store in dropper bottles.

Adult Dosage: 30–40 drops 3–4 times daily.

Child Dosage: 10–15 drops in tea or warm water.

Precautions:

- May slow absorption of medications—take them 1–2 hours apart.
- Safe for children and during pregnancy.

Licorice Root Adrenal & Lung Tincture

Function: Supports adrenal function, soothes sore throats, and aids lung health.

Ingredients:

- 1 cup dried licorice root
- 2.5 cups 40% alcohol or 60% glycerin

Instructions:

1. Combine ingredients in a jar, shake daily.

2. Let steep 4–6 weeks.
3. Strain and store in amber glass bottles.

Adult Dosage: 20–30 drops twice daily.

Child Dosage: 5–10 drops in warm tea or honey water.

Precautions:

- Avoid with high blood pressure or corticosteroids.
- Limit use to 2 weeks unless supervised.

Slippery Elm Digestive Soother Tincture

Function: Soothes irritation in the throat, esophagus, and intestines.

Ingredients:

- 1 cup powdered slippery elm bark
- 2.5 cups 60% glycerin + 40% water

Instructions:

1. Place powdered bark in a jar and add glycerin mix.
2. Shake daily for 4–6 weeks.
3. Strain thoroughly and bottle.

Adult Dosage: 30 drops before meals or during throat discomfort.

Child Dosage: 10–15 drops diluted in tea or juice.

Precautions:

- May impair absorption of medication—space out doses.
- Safe for children and pregnant women.

Fennel Digestive Carminative Tincture

Function: Reduces gas, bloating, and stomach discomfort.

Ingredients:

146

- 1 cup crushed dried fennel seeds
- 2.5 cups 40% vodka

Instructions:

1. Place fennel seeds in jar, cover with alcohol.
2. Label, shake daily for 4–6 weeks.
3. Strain and store in amber dropper bottles.

Adult Dosage: 20–30 drops after meals.

Child Dosage: 5–8 drops in tea or water.

Precautions:

- Avoid in estrogen-sensitive conditions.
- May support lactation in breastfeeding individuals.

Thyme Respiratory Tincture

Function: Expectorant, antimicrobial; great for coughs, colds, and bronchial infections.

Ingredients:

- 1 cup dried thyme
- 2.5 cups 40% alcohol or apple cider vinegar

Instructions:

1. Place thyme in a glass jar and cover with solvent.
2. Shake daily and steep for 4–6 weeks.
3. Strain and bottle in dark dropper jars.

Adult Dosage: 30 drops every 3–4 hours during illness.

Child Dosage: 10–12 drops in tea or warm water.

Precautions:

- Avoid in large doses during pregnancy.
- Not intended for long-term daily use.

Oregano Antiviral Tincture

Function: Potent antimicrobial; supports respiratory and gastrointestinal infections.

Ingredients:

- 1 cup dried oregano leaves
- 2.5 cups 60% alcohol

Instructions:

1. Place oregano leaves in a clean glass jar and cover with alcohol.
2. Seal, label, and store in a cool, dark place for 4–6 weeks.
3. Shake daily for full extraction.
4. Strain through fine mesh and bottle in amber dropper bottles.

Adult Dosage: 20–30 drops, 2–3 times daily during infection.

Child Dosage: 8–10 drops in honey or herbal tea, short-term use only.

Precautions:

- Can be too strong for children under 5.
- Avoid use during pregnancy; oregano can stimulate uterine contractions.

Rosemary Brain & Circulation Tincture

Function: Enhances mental clarity, memory, and circulation; antioxidant-rich.

Ingredients:

- 1 cup dried rosemary
- 2.5 cups 40% vodka

Instructions:

1. Place rosemary into a clean jar and cover with alcohol.
2. Shake daily and store in a dark location for 4–6 weeks.
3. Strain and store in dropper bottles.

Adult Dosage: 30 drops 2 times per day.

Child Dosage: 10–12 drops diluted in water or tea (age 8+).

Precautions:

- Avoid in epilepsy.
- Stimulating effect may disturb sleep if taken late.

Nettle Mineral-Rich Tonic Tincture

Function: Nutrient-dense; supports allergy relief, kidney function, and adrenal health.

Ingredients:

- 1 cup dried nettle leaf
- 2.5 cups 40% vodka or apple cider vinegar

Instructions:

1. Add nettle to a jar, pour in alcohol or vinegar.
2. Seal, label, and shake daily for 4–6 weeks.
3. Strain and store in amber glass bottles.

Adult Dosage: 30–40 drops 2 times daily.

Child Dosage: 10–15 drops in tea or juice.

Precautions:

- Diuretic—drink plenty of water.
- Generally safe for pregnancy in moderate amounts.

Red Raspberry Leaf Hormonal Tincture

Function: Tones the uterus, balances hormones, and supports pregnancy and menstrual cycles.

Ingredients:

- 1 cup dried red raspberry leaf
- 2.5 cups 40% vodka or apple cider vinegar

Instructions:

1. Place herb in jar and cover with solvent.
2. Label and shake daily for 4–6 weeks.
3. Strain and store in dropper bottles.

Adult Dosage: 30 drops 2 times daily.

Child Dosage: 10–12 drops for teens with menstrual symptoms.

Precautions:

- Avoid in early pregnancy unless supervised.
- Safe in 2nd and 3rd trimesters for uterine tone.

Dandelion Root Liver Detox Tincture

Function: Liver cleanser, digestive aid, supports bile production and skin health.

Ingredients:

1 cup dried or roasted dandelion root
2.5 cups 60% alcohol

Instructions:

1. Place root in jar and pour alcohol to cover completely.
2. Shake daily, store in a dark place for 4–6 weeks.
3. Strain through cloth and bottle.

Adult Dosage: 30 drops before meals.

Child Dosage: 10 drops diluted in warm water or juice.

Precautions:

- Avoid in gallbladder obstruction.
- May cause increased urination.

Burdock Root Skin & Blood Cleanser Tincture

Function: Purifies blood, supports lymphatic and liver function; useful for acne, eczema.

Ingredients:

- 1 cup dried burdock root
- 2.5 cups 60% alcohol

Instructions:

1. Combine ingredients in a jar, seal and shake daily.
2. Steep for 6 weeks in a dark space.
3. Strain and pour into amber bottles.

Adult Dosage: 30 drops twice daily.

Child Dosage: 8–10 drops diluted (for age 6+).

Precautions:

- Avoid during pregnancy.
- May increase urination; ensure hydration.

Hawthorn Heart Tonic Tincture

Function: Supports heart strength, improves circulation, and lowers blood pressure.

Ingredients:

- 1 cup dried hawthorn berries (or leaf/flower)
- 2.5 cups 40% vodka

Instructions:

1. Fill a jar with hawthorn and alcohol.
2. Shake daily and allow to extract for 4–6 weeks.
3. Strain and store in dropper bottles.

Adult Dosage: 30–40 drops 2–3 times daily for 3+ months.

Child Dosage: 10–12 drops in tea (age 10+).

Precautions:

- May interact with heart medications.
- Monitor blood pressure regularly when using long term.

Milk Thistle Liver Protector Tincture

Function: Regenerates liver cells, detoxifies liver, and protects from damage.

Ingredients:

- 1 cup crushed milk thistle seeds
- 2.5 cups 60% alcohol

Instructions:

1. Lightly crush seeds before soaking in alcohol.
2. Shake daily and store for 4–6 weeks.
3. Strain and pour into amber bottles.

Adult Dosage: 30–40 drops 2–3 times daily.

Child Dosage: 10 drops in juice or tea (age 6+).

Precautions:

- May affect medications metabolized by liver.
- Use under supervision with liver conditions.

Mullein Lung Support Tincture

Function: Soothes dry cough, strengthens lungs, and promotes expectoration.

Ingredients:

- 1 cup dried mullein leaves
- 2.5 cups 40% alcohol or glycerin

Instructions:

1. Place leaves in jar, cover with solvent.
2. Shake daily and store 4–6 weeks.
3. Filter through cloth or coffee filter to remove fine hairs.
4. Bottle in amber glass jars.

Adult Dosage: 30 drops every 3–4 hours for cough or congestion.

Child Dosage: 10–12 drops diluted in warm tea.

Precautions:

- Filter well—leaf hairs can irritate throat.
- Safe for use in pregnancy and children.

Elecampane Respiratory & Mucus Tincture

Function: Strong expectorant; clears mucus, relieves cough, and fights respiratory infections.

Ingredients:

- 1 cup dried elecampane root
- 2.5 cups 60% alcohol

Instructions:

1. Chop elecampane root and place in a glass jar.
2. Add alcohol to cover, seal, and label.
3. Shake daily for 4–6 weeks.
4. Strain thoroughly and store in dark bottles.

Adult Dosage: 30 drops up to 4 times daily for bronchial conditions.

Child Dosage: 10 drops with honey in warm water (age 6+).

Precautions:

- Limit to short-term use.
- Avoid during pregnancy.

🎓 Final Wisdom: The Art of Herbal Tincturing

Tinctures are more than just extracts—they are concentrated **relationships with the plant world**. Every bottle you make is a story: the gathering of ingredients, the waiting and shaking, the strain and pour, the intention and care.

When you prepare tinctures with attention, you're not just preserving a plant. You're **creating a legacy of healing**.

Chapter 10

Salves, Balms & Ointments

What's the Difference?

Salves, balms, and ointments are **semi-solid herbal preparations** made from infused oils, waxes, and therapeutic herbs that are **applied externally**. They're incredibly useful for treating skin conditions, sore muscles, minor wounds, bruises, and burns.

*"Note: Some herbalists choose to add a few drops of **essential oils** for added aroma or enhanced therapeutic effects. While not required, these can complement infused herbs beautifully. However, they are **optional** and can be **omitted entirely** for a more traditional, herbal-only blend"*

Term	Texture	Use Case
Salve	Soft, spreadable	Skin irritations, rashes, scrapes
Balm	Firmer, waxier	Lip care, cracked heels, protection
Ointment	Slightly greasier	Deep-tissue use, bruises, arthritis

Ointments are often greasier than salves because they typically contain a higher ratio of oil to wax and are absorbed more slowly into the skin. This makes them ideal for delivering herbs deeper into tissue, especially for joint issues, bruising, or protective layering over burns during the healing stage.

Infused Oils & Beeswax

What Are Infused Oils?

Infused oils are the **foundation** of most herbal salves, balms, and ointments. These are **carrier oils (like olive, coconut, or jojoba)** that have been steeped with dried herbs over time to absorb their healing properties.

Choosing Your Base Oils

Oil Type	Benefits
Olive Oil	Deeply moisturizing, stable shelf life
Coconut Oil	Antibacterial, firm texture
Jojoba Oil	Closest to skin's natural oils
Almond Oil	Lightweight, ideal for delicate skin
Sunflower Oil	High in Vitamin E

Top Herbs for Infused Oils

Herb	Action/Use
Calendula	Skin repair, inflammation
Comfrey	Speeds wound healing (use with care)
Plantain	Bug bites, stings, drawing action
Arnica	Bruising, muscle pain
Lavender	Antimicrobial, soothing
St. John's Wort	Nerve pain, sunburn relief
Chamomile	Anti-inflammatory, gentle for kids
Yarrow	Wound care, astringent

How to Make a Basic Herbal Infused Oil

There are **two main methods**: the **solar method (slow)** and the **heat method (quick)**.

☼ Solar Method (Cold Infusion – Recommended for Beginners)

1. Fill a clean jar about halfway with **dried herbs** (never fresh—fresh herbs spoil easily).
2. Cover completely with a carrier oil (e.g., olive oil), ensuring all herbs are submerged.
3. Stir with a clean utensil to remove air bubbles.

4. Seal and place in a warm, sunny window for **4–6 weeks**. Shake daily.
5. Strain through cheesecloth into a clean, dry jar. Label with herb name and date.

🔥 Heat Method (Double Boiler or Crockpot)

1. Place herbs and oil in a heat-safe glass jar or directly into a double boiler.
2. Heat gently for **3–6 hours** at no more than **100°F (38–40°C)**.
3. Stir occasionally and keep an eye on moisture.
4. Strain and store as above.

Tip: Always use dried herbs to prevent mold and spoilage.

Adding Beeswax to Make a Salve, Balm or Ointment

Beeswax gives your herbal oil **structure and shelf life**. The more beeswax, the **firmer** the final product.

Basic Salve, Balm or Ointment Formula

- 1 cup infused oil
- 1 oz (about 2 tablespoons) beeswax pellets or grated block

Instructions:

1. In a double boiler, warm the infused oil.
2. Add beeswax and stir until melted.
3. Test consistency: drop a spoonful on a plate. Let cool. Add more wax for firmness or more oil for softness.
4. Pour into **tins or jars** while warm. Let cool and label.

Optional Additions: Essential oils (e.g., lavender, tea tree), Vitamin E (preservative), menthol crystals (for cooling effect).

Skin, Pain, Bruise & Burn Blends

Here are **beginner-friendly herbal salve blends** for common skin conditions and external complaints. Each includes purpose, ingredients, and steps.

All-Purpose Healing Salve (Skin First Aid)

Use: Cuts, scrapes, rashes, eczema, bug bites.

Ingredients:

- ½ cup infused **calendula oil**
- ¼ cup infused **plantain oil**
- ¼ cup infused **chamomile oil**
- 1 oz beeswax
- 10 drops **lavender essential oil** (optional)

Instructions:

1. Combine infused oils in a double boiler.
2. Add beeswax, melt, and stir.
3. Remove from heat, stir in essential oil.
4. Pour into tins/jars and cool.

Pain & Joint Relief Balm

Use: Muscle tension, arthritis, deep aches.

Ingredients:

- ½ cup infused **arnica oil**
- ½ cup infused **St. John's Wort oil**
- 1 oz beeswax
- 10 drops **peppermint essential oil**
- 5 drops **eucalyptus essential oil**

Instructions:

1. Warm oils, melt in beeswax.
2. Stir in essential oils.
3. Pour and let cool.

⚠ **Do not use arnica on open wounds.**

Bruise & Bump Balm (For Kids + Adults)

Use: Minor bruises, sprains, contusions.

Ingredients:

- ½ cup infused **arnica oil**
- ¼ cup infused **comfrey oil**

- ¼ cup **coconut oil**
- 1 oz beeswax
- 10 drops **helichrysum essential oil** (optional)

Instructions:

1. Combine oils and melt with beeswax.
2. Pour into tins and allow to cool.
3. Apply 2–3x daily on unbroken skin.

Burn Soothing Ointment

Use: Minor kitchen burns, sunburn, chafing.

Ingredients:

- ½ cup infused **St. John's Wort oil**
- ½ cup infused **lavender oil**
- 1 oz beeswax
- 10 drops **lavender essential oil**

Instructions:

1. Gently warm oils and beeswax.
2. Add essential oil and stir.
3. Pour into wide-mouthed containers.
4. Apply to cooled, clean skin only.

⚠ Never apply oils to **fresh, open burns**—use **aloe vera gel first**, then switch to ointment during healing.

Lip Balm for Chapped or Cracked Lips

Use: Windburn, cracked lips, dry patches.

Ingredients:

- 2 tbsp **infused calendula oil**
- 2 tbsp **coconut oil**
- 1 tbsp **beeswax**
- 1–2 drops **peppermint or vanilla essential oil**

Instructions:

1. Melt oils and beeswax in a small pot.
2. Add scent oils if desired.
3. Pour into lip balm tubes or pots.

⚠ Safety Tips & Storage

- Always use **clean, dry containers**.
- Store in **cool, dark places**. Shelf life: 6–12 months.
- Don't apply to deep puncture wounds or infected skin without supervision.
- Patch test for allergies—especially with arnica or essential oils.
- Avoid comfrey on **open wounds** or during **pregnancy/nursing**.

---

40 Topical Recipes

"Note: Essential oils in these recipes are optional. Omit if you prefer a purely infused herbal preparation."

Calendula Skin Soothing Salve

Function: Soothes irritated, dry, or cracked skin. Supports healing of rashes and eczema.

Ingredients:

- 1/2 cup infused calendula oil
- 1/4 cup coconut oil
- 1 oz beeswax
- 10 drops lavender essential oil (optional)

Instructions:

1. Gently warm calendula and coconut oils in a double boiler.
2. Add beeswax and stir until fully melted.
3. Remove from heat, add lavender essential oil, stir well.
4. Pour into tins or jars, allow to cool and harden.
5. Label and store in a cool, dry place.

Usage:

Apply a thin layer to clean, dry skin 2–3 times daily or as needed.

Precautions:

- Avoid if allergic to plants in the Asteraceae (daisy) family.
- Do not use on deep or bleeding wounds.

Arnica Bruise & Sprain Balm

Function: Relieves bruising, muscle trauma, and minor sprains.

Ingredients:

- 1/2 cup infused arnica oil
- 1/4 cup comfrey-infused oil
- 1 oz beeswax
- 10 drops peppermint essential oil

Instructions:

1. Melt oils and beeswax in a double boiler over low heat.
2. Once beeswax is fully melted, remove from heat.
3. Stir in peppermint oil and mix thoroughly.
4. Pour into tins and let cool before sealing.

Usage:

Massage gently into bruised or sore areas 2–3 times daily.

Precautions:

- Do not apply to broken skin or open wounds.
- Arnica is for external use only—avoid ingestion.

Lavender Burn & Sun Relief Balm

Function: Cools and calms minor burns, sunburn, and inflammation.

Ingredients:

- 1/2 cup St. John's Wort infused oil
- 1/4 cup lavender-infused oil
- 1 oz beeswax

- 10 drops lavender essential oil

Instructions:

1. Gently warm oils and melt in beeswax.
2. Stir in lavender essential oil after removing from heat.
3. Pour into wide containers and let cool before use.

Usage:

Apply gently to minor burns or sun-exposed skin 2–3 times daily.

Precautions:

- Do not apply immediately after a fresh burn; wait until initial heat subsides.
- Avoid sun exposure directly after use—St. John's Wort may increase sun sensitivity.

Chamomile Baby Bum Balm

Function: Soothes diaper rash, skin redness, and baby eczema.

Ingredients:

- 1/2 cup chamomile-infused oil
- 1/4 cup calendula-infused oil
- 1/4 cup shea butter
- 1 oz beeswax

Instructions:

1. Melt oils, shea butter, and beeswax together over low heat.
2. Stir until completely liquified and uniform.
3. Pour into small jars or tins, allow to cool fully before closing.
4. Store in cool, dry environment.

Usage:

Apply a small amount to baby's clean bottom after diaper change or bath.

Precautions:

- Patch test on baby's arm first to check for sensitivity.
- For external use only—avoid eye or mouth contact.

Yarrow Antiseptic Wound Salve

Function: Antibacterial and astringent; aids healing of scrapes, cuts, and cracked skin.

Ingredients:

- 1/2 cup yarrow-infused oil
- 1/4 cup plantain-infused oil
- 1 oz beeswax
- 1 tsp vitamin E oil (optional)

Instructions:

1. Melt oils and beeswax together using a double boiler.
2. Add vitamin E oil if using, stir thoroughly.
3. Pour into sterilized containers and let cool.
4. Seal and label once firm.

Usage:

Apply to clean, minor cuts or abrasions 2 times per day.

Precautions:

- Avoid contact with deep or puncture wounds.
- Discontinue if irritation occurs; patch test first.

Nettle & Peppermint Joint Ease Balm

Function: Eases stiffness, swelling, and joint discomfort from arthritis or overuse.

Ingredients:

- 1/2 cup nettle-infused oil
- 1/4 cup peppermint-infused oil
- 1 oz beeswax
- 10 drops eucalyptus essential oil

Instructions:

1. Combine oils in a double boiler and gently heat.
2. Add beeswax and stir until melted completely.
3. Remove from heat, add eucalyptus oil, and mix well.
4. Pour into jars or tins and let cool.

Usage:

Massage gently into stiff or painful joints 2–3 times daily.

Precautions:

- Avoid contact with eyes and mucous membranes.
- Not for use on broken skin.

Plantain & Lavender Bug Bite Balm

Function: Reduces itching, swelling, and irritation from bug bites and stings.

Ingredients:

- 1/2 cup plantain-infused oil
- 1/4 cup lavender-infused oil
- 1 oz beeswax
- 10 drops tea tree essential oil

Instructions:

1. Melt oils and beeswax in a double boiler.
2. Remove from heat and add tea tree essential oil.
3. Pour into small containers, let cool and solidify.
4. Store in a cool, dark place.

Usage:

Apply directly to affected area 2–3 times per day.

Precautions:

- Avoid use near eyes or on sensitive genital areas.
- Patch test for essential oil sensitivity.

Rosemary Chest Vapor Rub

Function: Helps open airways, clear congestion, and soothe coughs.

Ingredients:

- 1/2 cup rosemary-infused oil
- 1/4 cup mullein-infused oil
- 1 oz beeswax
- 10 drops eucalyptus essential oil
- 5 drops peppermint essential oil

Instructions:

1. Gently melt oils and beeswax in a double boiler.
2. Add essential oils after removing from heat and stir well.
3. Pour into containers and let set before sealing.

Usage:

Rub on chest, back, or soles of feet during congestion or colds.

Precautions:

- Avoid applying near nose or mouth of infants or toddlers.
- Do not use if sensitive to strong aromas or menthol.

Thyme & Tea Tree Foot Balm

Function: Antifungal blend for athlete's foot, itchy toes, and cracked heels.

Ingredients:

- 1/2 cup thyme-infused oil
- 1/4 cup coconut oil
- 1 oz beeswax
- 10 drops tea tree essential oil
- 5 drops oregano essential oil (optional)

Instructions:

1. Combine all oils in a double boiler and gently warm.
2. Melt beeswax into the oils, then remove from heat.

3. Add essential oils, stir thoroughly, pour into tins.
4. Let cool and solidify completely before use.

Usage:

Apply to clean feet once or twice daily, especially between toes.

Precautions:

- Avoid contact with eyes or broken skin.
- Discontinue if irritation develops—essential oils are strong.

Comfrey Deep Tissue Ointment

Function: Penetrates deeply to support healing of strains, sprains, and bone bruises.

Ingredients:

- 1/2 cup comfrey-infused oil
- 1/4 cup arnica-infused oil
- 1 oz beeswax
- 10 drops ginger essential oil (optional)

Instructions:

1. Melt oils and beeswax together over low heat.
2. Add ginger essential oil after removing from heat.
3. Stir well, pour into containers, and allow to cool.
4. Label and store away from heat.

Usage:

Massage into affected area 2–3 times per day.

Precautions:

- Not for use on open wounds or broken skin.
- Avoid during pregnancy and breastfeeding without guidance.

Lemon Balm Cold Sore Lip Salve

Function: Soothes and shortens the duration of cold sores and lip irritation.

Ingredients:

- 1/2 cup lemon balm-infused oil
- 1/4 cup coconut oil
- 1 oz beeswax
- 5 drops tea tree essential oil
- 5 drops lavender essential oil

Instructions:

1. Warm oils and beeswax in a double boiler over low heat.
2. Once fully melted, stir in essential oils and mix thoroughly.
3. Pour into lip balm tubes or small jars.
4. Allow to cool and label containers.

Usage:

Apply directly to cold sore or dry lips as needed, especially at onset.

Precautions:

- For external lip use only.
- Discontinue if skin irritation occurs.

Slippery Elm Skin Repair Ointment

Function: Promotes healing of dry, cracked skin and minor wounds.

Ingredients:

- 1/2 cup slippery elm-infused oil
- 1/4 cup calendula-infused oil
- 1 oz beeswax
- 1 tsp vitamin E oil

Instructions:

1. Gently heat infused oils and beeswax until fully melted.
2. Stir in vitamin E oil thoroughly.

3. Pour into containers and let cool.
4. Store in a cool, dry place.

Usage:

Apply to dry, cracked, or healing skin 2 times daily.

Precautions:

- Avoid use on deep wounds.
- External use only; not for internal mucosa.

Holy Basil (Tulsi) Stress Relief Balm

Function: Relieves tension and supports emotional calm when applied to temples or chest.

Ingredients:

- 1/2 cup holy basil-infused oil
- 1/4 cup lavender-infused oil
- 1 oz beeswax
- 5 drops frankincense essential oil
- 5 drops lavender essential oil

Instructions:

1. Warm oils and beeswax together until melted.
2. Add essential oils, mix well, and pour into small balm containers.
3. Cool and label properly.

Usage:

Rub on temples, neck, or chest during stressful moments.

Precautions:

- Avoid contact with eyes.
- Do not use during pregnancy without medical guidance.

Milk Thistle Liver Rub Balm

Function: Applied over the liver area to support detox pathways and mild lymphatic drainage.

Ingredients:

- 1/2 cup milk thistle-infused oil
- 1/4 cup dandelion-infused oil
- 1 oz beeswax
- 10 drops rosemary essential oil

Instructions:

1. Heat oils and beeswax together in a double boiler.
2. Remove from heat and stir in rosemary essential oil.
3. Pour into tins and allow to harden.
4. Label and store away from sunlight.

Usage:

Apply over liver area (upper right abdomen) 1–2 times daily.

Precautions:

- External use only.
- Not a substitute for medical detox protocols.

Red Raspberry Leaf Breast Balm

Function: Tones and nourishes breast tissue; traditionally used postpartum and during lactation.

Ingredients:

- 1/2 cup red raspberry leaf-infused oil
- 1/4 cup calendula-infused oil
- 1 oz beeswax
- 5 drops geranium essential oil

Instructions:

1. Gently melt oils and beeswax in a double boiler.

2. Add geranium oil once cooled slightly, stir well.
3. Pour into tins and let solidify completely.
4. Label and store in cool, dry area.

Usage:

Massage a small amount into breast tissue 1–2 times daily.

Precautions:

- Avoid application directly before nursing.
- Discontinue use if any nipple or skin irritation occurs.

Licorice Root Eczema Relief Balm

Function: Soothes inflamed skin and reduces itching caused by eczema and dermatitis.

Ingredients:

- 1/2 cup licorice root-infused oil
- 1/4 cup calendula-infused oil
- 1 oz beeswax
- 5 drops lavender essential oil

Instructions:

1. Melt oils and beeswax gently in a double boiler.
2. Remove from heat and stir in essential oil.
3. Pour into containers and allow to cool.
4. Label and store in a dry, shaded place.

Usage:

Apply a thin layer to affected areas 2–3 times daily.

Precautions:

- Avoid contact with open wounds or eyes.
- Not recommended for long-term use on large skin areas.

Valerian Nerve Soothe Balm

Function: Eases nerve-related pain, such as tension, sciatica, or nighttime restlessness.

Ingredients:

- 1/2 cup valerian root-infused oil
- 1/4 cup St. John's Wort-infused oil
- 1 oz beeswax
- 5 drops chamomile essential oil (optional)

Instructions:

1. Gently heat infused oils and beeswax until melted.
2. Add essential oil, stir thoroughly.
3. Pour into small jars or balm containers and let set.
4. Label and store in cool, dark location.

Usage:

Massage into lower back, neck, or feet before bedtime.

Precautions:

- May cause drowsiness—use only at night.
- Not for pregnant or nursing women.

Echinacea Skin Defense Salve

Function: Supports natural immune defense and promotes skin healing for minor wounds.

Ingredients:

- 1/2 cup echinacea-infused oil
- 1/4 cup plantain-infused oil
- 1 oz beeswax
- 1 tsp vitamin E oil

Instructions:

1. Warm infused oils and beeswax in a double boiler.
2. Add vitamin E oil and mix thoroughly.

3. Pour into jars or tins, allow to cool.
4. Label with name and date.

Usage:

Apply to minor cuts and scrapes 1–2 times daily.

Precautions:

- For external use only.
- Do not use on infected or weeping wounds.

Burdock & Nettle Rash Relief Salve

Function: Cleanses and calms skin affected by rashes, acne, or hives.

Ingredients:

- 1/2 cup burdock root-infused oil
- 1/4 cup nettle-infused oil
- 1 oz beeswax
- 5 drops tea tree essential oil

Instructions:

1. Melt oils and beeswax together until uniform.
2. Remove from heat and stir in essential oil.
3. Pour into clean jars or tins and allow to set.
4. Store away from sunlight.

Usage:

Apply gently to rash-prone or inflamed skin 2 times daily.

Precautions:

- Avoid broken or bleeding skin.
- Patch test before widespread use.

Ginger & St. John's Wort Nerve Pain Balm

Function: Soothes sciatic nerve discomfort and deep aching pain.

Ingredients:

- 1/2 cup St. John's Wort-infused oil
- 1/4 cup ginger-infused oil
- 1 oz beeswax
- 5 drops peppermint essential oil

Instructions:

1. Warm infused oils and beeswax over low heat.
2. Stir in peppermint oil once removed from heat.
3. Pour into containers and let solidify.
4. Store in a dark, cool place.

Usage:

Massage into painful areas 2–3 times per day.

Precautions:

- Do not apply before sun exposure—photosensitivity risk from St. John's Wort.
- Avoid mucous membranes and eyes.

Skullcap Tension Relief Balm

Function: Helps reduce tension headaches and jaw tightness when applied topically.

Ingredients:

- 1/2 cup skullcap-infused oil
- 1/4 cup lavender-infused oil
- 1 oz beeswax
- 5 drops peppermint essential oil

Instructions:

1. Gently melt oils and beeswax in a double boiler.
2. Remove from heat and stir in peppermint essential oil.
3. Pour into jars and let cool.

4. Store in a dark, dry place.

Usage:

Massage gently onto temples, neck, and shoulders.

Precautions:

- Avoid contact with eyes.
- Do not use on broken skin.

Marshmallow Root Moisture Balm

Function: Deeply hydrates dry or chapped skin; great for hands and feet.

Ingredients:

- 1/2 cup marshmallow root-infused oil
- 1/4 cup shea butter
- 1 oz beeswax
- 5 drops chamomile essential oil

Instructions:

1. Combine infused oil, shea butter, and beeswax in a double boiler.
2. Melt gently until smooth, then remove from heat.
3. Stir in essential oil, pour into tins, and allow to harden.
4. Store away from direct sunlight.

Usage:

Apply to dry skin areas as needed throughout the day.

Precautions:

- External use only.
- Test on small area if sensitive skin is a concern.

Mullein Chest Comfort Balm

Function: Soothes chest tightness and supports easier breathing during colds.

Ingredients:

- 1/2 cup mullein-infused oil
- 1/4 cup eucalyptus-infused oil
- 1 oz beeswax
- 10 drops camphor essential oil

Instructions:

1. Melt oils and beeswax together using a double boiler.
2. Stir in camphor oil after removing from heat.
3. Pour into wide jars or tins and cool.
4. Seal and store in a dry place.

Usage:

Apply to chest and upper back 2–3 times daily.

Precautions:

- Do not use on babies or small children.
- Avoid contact with face or mucous membranes.

Chamomile & Lemon Balm Sleep Balm

Function: Encourages relaxation and restful sleep when massaged into pulse points.

Ingredients:

- 1/2 cup chamomile-infused oil
- 1/4 cup lemon balm-infused oil
- 1 oz beeswax
- 5 drops lavender essential oil

Instructions:

1. Melt all ingredients (except essential oil) gently over low heat.
2. Remove from heat, stir in lavender oil, and blend thoroughly.
3. Pour into small containers and allow to set.
4. Label clearly for nighttime use.

Usage:

Rub into temples, wrists, and neck before bedtime.

Precautions:

- Use only before rest periods due to sedative effects.
- Not for use on infants or very young children.

Yarrow Menstrual Cramp Balm

Function: Relieves cramping and tension in the lower abdomen during menstruation.

Ingredients:

- 1/2 cup yarrow-infused oil
- 1/4 cup ginger-infused oil
- 1 oz beeswax
- 5 drops clary sage essential oil

Instructions:

1. Heat oils and beeswax until fully melted.
2. Stir in clary sage essential oil after removing from heat.
3. Pour into jars and allow to cool completely.
4. Store in a cool, dry cabinet.

Usage:

Massage into lower belly 2–3 times per day during cycle.

Precautions:

- Avoid use during pregnancy.
- Do not apply to broken skin.

Dandelion Muscle Ease Balm

Function: Relieves sore, tight muscles and promotes circulation post-activity.

Ingredients:

- 1/2 cup dandelion-infused oil
- 1/4 cup arnica-infused oil
- 1 oz beeswax
- 10 drops black pepper essential oil

Instructions:

1. Warm oils and beeswax in a double boiler until fully melted.
2. Stir in essential oil after removing from heat.
3. Pour into containers and allow to cool.
4. Label clearly and store in a cool place.

Usage:

Massage into sore muscles after exercise or strenuous activity.

Precautions:

- Avoid using on inflamed or broken skin.
- External use only—keep away from eyes and mouth.

Hawthorn Heart Rub Balm

Function: Traditionally applied over the chest area for energetic heart support.

Ingredients:

- 1/2 cup hawthorn-infused oil
- 1/4 cup rose-infused oil
- 1 oz beeswax
- 5 drops rose essential oil

Instructions:

1. Melt beeswax and oils together on low heat.
2. Add essential oil once cooled slightly and stir well.
3. Pour into balm tins and cool completely before sealing.
4. Label for topical heart support use.

Usage:

Rub gently over chest or heart center 1–2 times daily.

Precautions:

- Not a substitute for cardiac medical care.
- Do not apply near eyes or mucous membranes.

Sage & Thyme Warming Foot Balm

Function: Boosts circulation and warmth in cold feet; helps combat fungal buildup.

Ingredients:

- 1/2 cup sage-infused oil
- 1/4 cup thyme-infused oil
- 1 oz beeswax
- 10 drops cinnamon essential oil

Instructions:

1. Combine and melt oils with beeswax in double boiler.
2. Remove from heat and stir in essential oil.
3. Pour into tins and let harden at room temperature.
4. Store away from sunlight.

Usage:

Massage into feet at bedtime or after showers.

Precautions:

- Avoid use on sensitive skin or open cuts.
- Patch test before full use—warming oils can be strong.

Elderflower Skin Brightening Balm

Function: Tones and rejuvenates dull, uneven skin; traditionally used on face and neck.

Ingredients:

- 1/2 cup elderflower-infused oil
- 1/4 cup calendula-infused oil
- 1 oz beeswax

- 5 drops frankincense essential oil

Instructions:

1. Gently melt oils and beeswax over low heat.
2. Add frankincense oil, stir well, and pour into containers.
3. Let cool completely before capping.
4. Label clearly and refrigerate if in hot climates.

Usage:

Apply lightly to clean skin on face or neck before bedtime.

Precautions:

- Avoid getting into eyes.
- Discontinue use if any irritation develops.

Linden Flower Calming Balm

Function: Eases anxiety and supports emotional regulation when applied to pulse points.

Ingredients:

- 1/2 cup linden flower-infused oil
- 1/4 cup holy basil-infused oil
- 1 oz beeswax
- 5 drops neroli or orange essential oil

Instructions:

1. Melt infused oils and beeswax in a double boiler.
2. Remove from heat and stir in essential oil.
3. Pour into balm jars and let set completely.
4. Label with name and intended calming use.

Usage:

Rub gently into wrists, temples, or chest as needed during anxious moments.

Precautions:

- For aromatic topical use only.

- Avoid contact with eyes or sensitive skin.

Calendula & Marshmallow Dry Skin Salve

Function: Deeply hydrates cracked, irritated, or winter-dry skin.

Ingredients:

- 1/2 cup calendula-infused oil
- 1/4 cup marshmallow root-infused oil
- 1 oz beeswax
- 5 drops chamomile essential oil

Instructions:

1. Melt oils and beeswax over low heat.
2. Remove from heat and stir in essential oil.
3. Pour into containers and let cool.

Usage:

Apply 2–3 times daily to dry or inflamed areas.

Precautions:

For external use only. Discontinue if rash occurs.

Comfrey & Lavender Healing Salve

Function: Accelerates healing for scrapes, bruises, and inflammation.

Ingredients:

- 1/2 cup comfrey-infused oil
- 1/4 cup lavender-infused oil
- 1 oz beeswax
- 10 drops lavender essential oil

Instructions:

1. Gently heat oils and beeswax until melted.

2. Add essential oil and mix well.
3. Pour into small tins or jars and let set.

Usage:

Apply thin layer on clean skin.

Precautions:

Do not use on open wounds or during pregnancy.

Chickweed Itch Relief Salve

Function: Relieves itching from eczema, hives, and allergic rashes.

Ingredients:

- 1/2 cup chickweed-infused oil
- 1/4 cup plantain-infused oil
- 1 oz beeswax

Instructions:

1. Warm oils and beeswax, stirring until melted.
2. Pour into jars, allow to cool.

Usage:

Use on itchy, irritated skin as needed.

Precautions:

For external use only. Patch test before full use.

Violet Leaf Anti-Inflammatory Salve

Function: Cools inflammation from skin flare-ups or hot, swollen areas.

Ingredients:

- 1/2 cup violet leaf-infused oil

- 1/4 cup coconut oil
- 1 oz beeswax

Instructions:

1. Melt oils and beeswax over gentle heat.
2. Stir thoroughly and pour into tins.

Usage:

Apply to warm, red, inflamed skin twice daily.

Precautions:

Discontinue if irritation worsens.

Goldenseal Antimicrobial Skin Salve

Function: Helps prevent infection in minor cuts and insect bites.

Ingredients:

- 1/2 cup goldenseal root-infused oil
- 1/4 cup olive oil
- 1 oz beeswax

Instructions:

1. Heat oils with beeswax until blended.
2. Pour into sterilized jars, label and cool.

Usage:

Dab onto minor wounds or insect stings.

Precautions:

External use only. Not for use during pregnancy.

Turmeric Joint Relief Ointment

Function: Reduces inflammation and supports joint mobility.

Ingredients

- 1/2 cup turmeric root-infused oil
- 1/4 cup ginger-infused oil
- 1 oz beeswax
- 5 drops black pepper essential oil

Instructions:

1. Warm oils and beeswax until melted.
2. Stir in essential oil.
3. Pour into jars and allow to cool.

Usage:

Massage into joints as needed.

Precautions:

May stain clothing. Avoid contact with eyes.

Solomon's Seal Ligament & Tendon Ointment

Function: Supports healing of ligament strains and connective tissue damage.

Ingredients:

- 1/2 cup Solomon's seal-infused oil
- 1/4 cup arnica-infused oil
- 1 oz beeswax

Instructions:

1. Melt oils and beeswax together.
2. Pour into containers and cool.

Usage:

Rub gently into affected area twice daily.

Precautions:

Not for use on open skin. Avoid during pregnancy.

Myrrh & Frankincense Healing Ointment

Function: Traditionally used for skin healing, cracked heels, and spiritual anointing.

Ingredients:

1/2 cup myrrh-infused oil
1/4 cup frankincense-infused oil
1 oz beeswax

Instructions:

1. Heat ingredients in a double boiler.
2. Stir thoroughly and pour into jars.

Usage:

Apply sparingly to skin or pulse points.

Precautions:

Not for use during pregnancy or on sensitive areas.

Usnea Antifungal Ointment

Function: Fights fungal infections on skin or nails.

Ingredients:

- 1/2 cup usnea-infused oil
- 1/4 cup coconut oil
- 1 oz beeswax
- 5 drops tea tree essential oil

Instructions:

1. Warm oils and beeswax.
2. Add essential oil, pour into ointment jars.

Usage:

Apply to fungal-affected areas 1–2 times daily.

Precautions:

Patch test for sensitivity. Avoid eyes and mucous membranes.

Ginger & Mustard Circulation Ointment

Function: Stimulates blood flow for cold extremities or sluggish circulation.

Ingredients:

- 1/2 cup ginger-infused oil
- 1/4 cup mustard seed-infused oil
- 1 oz beeswax
- 5 drops rosemary essential oil

Instructions:

1. Melt all ingredients gently.
2. Stir and pour into wide-mouth jars.

Usage:

Rub into hands, feet, or low-back areas as needed.

Precautions:

Avoid broken skin. May feel warming—patch test before full use.

Final Thoughts…

Creating herbal salves and balms is **simple, satisfying, and empowering**. It connects you with traditional healing methods while giving you control over your skincare and first-aid products. Start with 1–2 infused oils, explore their effects, and then blend more complex formulas as you grow in confidence.

Chapter 11

Culinary Herbalism

Culinary herbalism is the art and science of using herbs not just for healing teas or topical remedies, but as vibrant ingredients in everyday cooking. It's one of the most delicious and accessible ways to integrate herbal wellness into your life — meal by meal, bite by bite.

It is one of the oldest forms of plant medicine, practiced in every traditional culture where food and health were inseparable. In this chapter, you'll discover how to use **herbs as food and flavor**, turning your kitchen into a daily apothecary.

Whether you're sprinkling dried thyme on roasted vegetables or infusing vinegar with nettle for salad dressings, these recipes are about **gentle, daily herbal support** — not just for treating illness but for **staying well every day**.

Why Culinary Herbalism Matters

Unlike isolated herbal doses, culinary herbalism offers a *gentle, sustained infusion of plant medicine* into your body through food. This method is especially supportive for:

- **Preventative wellness** (e.g., supporting digestion, immunity, detoxification)
- **Long-term resilience** (building gut health, reducing inflammation)
- **Flavor-enhanced healing** (herbs make everything taste better while helping your body!)

Herbal Vinegars, Butters & Seasonings

These are foundational staples of culinary herbalism. They're simple to make, highly versatile, and packed with healing potential. They're ideal entry points into herbalism for beginners.

Herbal Vinegars

Herbal vinegars are tangy, mineral-rich infusions made by soaking herbs in vinegar. You can use them:

- In salad dressings
- As a deglazing liquid for sautéed dishes
- Added to bone broths

- Diluted as a daily "tonic shot"

Best Vinegars to Use:

- **Raw Apple Cider Vinegar**: Nutrient-rich and probiotic
- **Red or White Wine Vinegar**: Great for culinary elegance
- **Rice Vinegar**: Mild, slightly sweet

How to Make Herbal Vinegar (Step-by-Step):

1. Choose your herbs (fresh or dried). Avoid moldy or damp herbs.
2. Fill a clean glass jar ½ to ¾ full with the herb(s).
3. Pour vinegar over herbs to completely cover them.
4. Seal tightly (use plastic lids or cover metal with parchment to avoid corrosion).
5. Label with the date and contents.
6. Shake daily and store in a cool, dark place for 2–4 weeks.
7. Strain through cheesecloth and transfer to a clean bottle.

Popular Combinations:

- **Bone-Building Vinegar**: Nettle, red clover, oatstraw
- **Digestion Boost**: Rosemary, lemon balm, sage
- **Cold & Flu Blend**: Thyme, garlic, elderflower

Tips:

- For culinary use, strain well to remove floating herbs.
- Store in a glass bottle in the pantry for up to 1 year.

Herbal Butters (or Vegan Spreads)

These are compound butters made by blending fresh or dried herbs into soft butter. Use them to:

- Spread on toast, crackers, cornbread
- Melt over grilled veggies or meats
- Add to mashed potatoes, rice, or pasta

Base Recipe:

1. Let ½ cup of **unsalted butter** (or ghee/coconut oil) soften at room temperature.
2. Finely chop 2–4 tablespoons of **herbs** (fresh preferred, dried optional).
3. Add pinch of salt, lemon zest, garlic, or honey depending on use.
4. Mix until well combined.

5. Roll into a log using parchment paper or pack into ramekins.
6. Chill for at least 2 hours before serving.

Favorite Variations:

- **Herbal Garlic Butter**: Parsley, chive, thyme, garlic
- **Relaxing Lavender-Honey Butter**: Lavender flowers, raw honey
- **Digestive Butter**: Fennel seed, peppermint, lemon balm

Storage: Keeps 1–2 weeks refrigerated or can be frozen.

Herbal Seasoning Blends

These dry blends are ready-to-use flavor enhancers that double as **daily health boosters**. They're cheaper, cleaner, and more tailored than commercial versions.

How to Make:

1. Choose dried herbs only.
2. Blend by hand or pulse in a spice grinder.
3. Store in a clean, dry jar.

Common Ratios:

- 1 part strong flavor (e.g., rosemary, oregano)
- 2 parts milder flavor (e.g., parsley, thyme)
- Optional: add dried citrus peel, garlic powder, or cayenne

Sample Blends:

- **Italian Vitality Mix**: Basil, oregano, thyme, rosemary
- **Calm the Belly Mix**: Fennel, coriander, peppermint
- **Sweet Spice Mix**: Cinnamon, ginger, cardamom (great for oatmeal or baked goods)

Pro Tip: Add **nutritional yeast** or **ground sesame seeds** for minerals and umami flavor!

---

36 Edible Herbal Recipes

These recipes make it easy to incorporate herbs into everyday meals. All are designed to be **simple, repeatable, and flexible**.

Mineral-Rich Herbal Broth

Function: Nourishes deeply with minerals and adaptogens; supports immune strength, detox pathways, and overall vitality.

Ingredients:

- 1/4 cup dried nettle
- 2 tbsp dandelion root
- 1 tbsp burdock root
- 1 tbsp astragalus root
- 1 onion, chopped
- 1 garlic bulb, halved
- 10 cups water
- Salt and pepper

Instructions:

1. Combine all in a large pot.
2. Simmer gently for 1–2 hours.
3. Strain and store broth for up to 5 days.

How to Use:

Use as a nourishing base for soups, grains, stews, or sip warm between meals with a spoon of miso.

Precautions:

- Not recommended for individuals with kidney concerns or who are on potassium-restricted diets.

- Use organic herbs when possible to avoid contaminants.

Herbal Salad Dressing

Function: Supports digestion and immunity; delivers antioxidants and minerals from infused herbs in an everyday format.

Ingredients:

- 1/4 cup herbal vinegar
- 1/2 cup olive oil
- 1 tbsp honey or maple syrup
- 1 tsp mustard
- 1 tsp dried oregano
- Salt and black pepper

Instructions:

1. Combine all in a jar and shake well.
2. Store in fridge for up to 10 days.

How to Use:

Drizzle over salads, roasted veggies, or grain bowls for a health-boosting dressing.

Precautions:

- Vinegar may aggravate acid reflux in sensitive individuals.
- Store refrigerated and discard if cloudy or bubbling.

Immune Chimichurri

Function: Rich in antimicrobial and antioxidant properties; supports detox and immune balance.

Ingredients:

- 1 cup parsley
- 1/2 cup oregano
- 1/2 cup olive oil
- 3 garlic cloves
- 2 tbsp apple cider vinegar
- Sea salt, chili flakes

Instructions:

1. Blend all ingredients until smooth.
2. Use over grilled vegetables, meats, or grains.

How to Use:

Spoon generously over warm dishes or use as a vibrant dip or marinade.

Precautions:

- Garlic may interact with blood-thinning medications—use moderately.
- Store refrigerated and consume within 5 days.

Nettle Sesame Sprinkle

Function: High in minerals like calcium, iron, and iodine; supports energy, bone strength, and thyroid health.

Ingredients:

- 2 tbsp dried nettle
- 2 tbsp sesame seeds
- 1 tbsp parsley
- 1 tbsp dulse flakes (optional)
- 1 tsp sea salt

Instructions:

1. Blend or crush in mortar until flaky.
2. Store in a glass shaker jar.

How to Use:

Sprinkle on toast, soup, rice, or eggs for added nutrition and flavor.

Precautions:

- Nettle may act as a diuretic—monitor use with medications.
- Dulse is high in iodine—use cautiously with thyroid conditions.

Herbal Egg Blend

Function: A digestive-supporting, anti-inflammatory seasoning blend for daily breakfast use.

Ingredients:

- 1 tbsp dried basil
- 1 tbsp chive
- 1 tsp turmeric
- 1 tsp thyme

- Salt and black pepper

How to Use:

Add 1 tsp of this dry mix per 2 eggs for scrambles or omelets.

Precautions:

- Turmeric may interfere with gallbladder issues or blood thinners—use moderately.
- Store in an airtight container away from light.

Gut-Soothing Herbal Ghee

Function: Supports digestion and soothes the gut; ideal for weak digestion or post-antibiotic care.

Ingredients:

- 1/2 cup ghee
- 1 tsp fennel seed
- 1 tsp ginger powder

- 1 tsp cumin seed

Instructions:

1. Heat ghee on low heat.
2. Add spices and cook 2–3 minutes.
3. Cool and store.

How to Use:

Stir into warm rice, spread on toast, or use to sauté greens.

Precautions:

- Not suitable for dairy-intolerant individuals unless using clarified ghee.
- Use moderate amounts if on a low-fat diet.

Nettle & Garlic Mineral Pesto

Function: Rich in minerals like iron and calcium; supports energy and bone health.

Ingredients:

- 1 cup blanched nettle leaves
- 1/2 cup parsley
- 1/4 cup toasted sunflower seeds
- 3 garlic cloves

- 1/2 cup olive oil
- 1/4 cup grated parmesan (optional)
- Juice of 1 lemon
- Salt to taste

Instructions:

1. Blanch nettles in boiling water for 1 minute, then plunge into cold water and squeeze dry.
2. Combine all ingredients in a food processor.
3. Blend until smooth, adjusting oil and salt to taste.
4. Store in the fridge up to 5 days or freeze in small portions.

How to Use:

Use as a spread on bread, stir into pasta, or serve with roasted vegetables.

Precautions:

- Wear gloves when handling raw nettle to avoid stings.
- Not recommended for individuals with kidney issues without supervision.

Lemon Balm Herbal Lemonade

Function: Calms the nervous system and uplifts mood; supports digestion.

Ingredients:

- 1/2 cup fresh lemon balm leaves
- 1/4 cup honey (or to taste)
- 1/2 cup fresh lemon juice
- 4 cups cold water
- Lemon slices (optional)

Instructions:

1. Bruise lemon balm leaves gently to release oils.
2. In a pitcher, combine lemon balm, honey, and lemon juice.
3. Add water and stir until honey dissolves.
4. Chill and serve with lemon slices if desired.

How to Use:

Serve cold on warm days to soothe stress or as a calming daily beverage.

Precautions:

Lemon balm may lower thyroid activity; monitor if on thyroid medication.

Thyme Immune Soup Base

Function: Supports respiratory health and boosts the immune system.

Ingredients:

- 1 onion, chopped

- 2 cloves garlic, minced
- 1 tsp dried thyme
- 1 tsp dried oregano
- 1 bay leaf
- 8 cups vegetable or chicken broth
- Salt and pepper to taste

Instructions:

1. Sauté onion and garlic until translucent.
2. Add herbs and stir for 1 minute.
3. Add broth, bring to a simmer, and cook 20 minutes.
4. Strain or use as is for soups.

How to Use:

Use as a healing soup base or sip warm when feeling under the weather.

Precautions:

- Avoid excessive thyme intake during pregnancy.
- Use moderate salt if hypertensive.

Tulsi (Holy Basil) Tea Infusion

Function: Adaptogenic herb that reduces stress and supports immune health.

Ingredients:

- 2 tbsp dried tulsi (holy basil) leaves
- 2 cups boiling water
- Honey or lemon (optional)

Instructions:

1. Pour boiling water over tulsi leaves in a teapot.
2. Steep for 10–15 minutes covered.
3. Strain and sweeten if desired.

How to Use:

Drink 1–2 cups daily as a calming ritual or during periods of stress.

Precautions:

May affect blood sugar and blood thinning medications.

Rosemary & Sage Roasted Potatoes

Function: Supports memory, digestion, and adds antioxidant power.

Ingredients:

- 1.5 lbs potatoes, cubed
- 2 tbsp olive oil
- 1 tsp dried rosemary
- 1 tsp dried sage
- Salt and black pepper to taste

Instructions:

1. Preheat oven to 400°F (200°C).
2. Toss potatoes with oil, herbs, salt, and pepper.
3. Spread on a baking sheet.
4. Roast for 30–40 minutes until golden and crisp.

How to Use:

Serve as a side dish or snack, especially during colder months.

Precautions:

Use herbs in moderation if on blood pressure medications.

Chamomile Honey Oat Cookies

Function: Soothes the nervous system and aids restful sleep.

Ingredients:

- 1/2 cup butter or coconut oil
- 1/2 cup honey
- 1 egg
- 1 tsp vanilla extract
- 1 cup rolled oats
- 3/4 cup whole wheat flour
- 2 tbsp dried chamomile flowers (ground)
- 1/2 tsp baking soda
- Pinch of salt

Instructions:

1. Preheat oven to 350°F (175°C).
2. Cream butter and honey until smooth, then add egg and vanilla.
3. Mix in oats, flour, baking soda, salt, and ground chamomile.
4. Scoop onto parchment-lined baking sheet.
5. Bake 10–12 minutes or until golden.

How to Use:

Enjoy 1–2 cookies in the evening to help relax and unwind.

Precautions:

Avoid chamomile if allergic to ragweed or daisies.

Calendula Rice Pilaf

Function: Supports skin health and gentle detoxification.

Ingredients:

- 1 cup long grain rice
- 2 cups vegetable broth
- 1 tbsp olive oil
- 1/4 cup dried calendula petals
- 1/2 onion, chopped
- 1 garlic clove, minced
- Salt and pepper to taste

Instructions:

1. Sauté onion and garlic in olive oil until soft.
2. Add rice and stir to coat.
3. Pour in broth and bring to boil.
4. Stir in calendula petals.
5. Cover, reduce heat, and simmer for 18–20 minutes.

How to Use:

Serve as a colorful side dish or base for stews and vegetables.

Precautions:

Calendula is generally safe but avoid internal use during pregnancy without professional guidance.

Garlic & Sage Immune Hummus

Function: Antimicrobial and supportive to respiratory health.

Ingredients:

- 1 can chickpeas (15 oz), drained
- 2 tbsp tahini
- 2 cloves garlic
- 1 tsp dried sage
- Juice of 1 lemon
- 2 tbsp olive oil
- Salt to taste

Instructions:

1. Combine all ingredients in a food processor.
2. Blend until creamy, adding water as needed.
3. Adjust seasonings to taste.

How to Use:

Use as a spread on sandwiches or as a dip with vegetables.

Precautions:

Garlic may cause digestive upset in sensitive individuals.

Dandelion Detox Smoothie

Function: Liver and kidney detoxifier; aids digestion and skin clarity.

Ingredients:

- 1 cup dandelion greens
- 1 banana
- 1/2 avocado
- 1/2 lemon, juiced
- 1 cup coconut water
- 1/2 tsp spirulina (optional)

Instructions:

1. Add all ingredients to a blender.
2. Blend until smooth.
3. Serve immediately.

How to Use:

Drink in the morning or after heavy meals for digestive support.

Precautions:

Dandelion greens may be bitter and can stimulate bile; start with a small amount.

Lavender Rose Herbal Sugar

Function: Uplifts mood, calms the nervous system, and beautifies desserts.

Ingredients:

- 1 cup organic cane sugar
- 2 tsp dried lavender buds
- 1 tbsp dried rose petals

Instructions:

1. Grind herbs in a spice grinder or crush finely.
2. Mix into sugar until evenly blended.
3. Store in airtight jar for up to 3 months.

How to Use:

Use in baking, tea, or to rim cocktail/mocktail glasses.

Precautions:

- Use edible, pesticide-free flowers only.
- Lavender in excess may cause drowsiness.

Fennel & Mint Digestive Tea

Function: Relieves bloating, gas, and digestive discomfort after meals.

Ingredients:

- 1 tsp fennel seeds
- 1 tsp dried peppermint leaves
- 1/2 tsp dried ginger (optional)
- 2 cups boiling water

Instructions:

1. Place herbs in a teapot or infuser.
2. Pour boiling water over and steep 10–15 minutes.
3. Strain before serving.

How to Use:

Drink 1 cup after meals to ease digestion and reduce gas.

Precautions:

- Fennel may interact with estrogen-sensitive conditions.
- Peppermint may worsen acid reflux in some individuals.

Cilantro Detox Chimichurri

Function: Supports heavy metal detox, liver function, and digestion.

Ingredients:

- 1 cup fresh cilantro
- 1/2 cup parsley
- 2 garlic cloves
- 1/4 cup olive oil
- 1 tbsp lemon juice
- Salt and pepper to taste

Instructions:

1. Blend all ingredients in a food processor until smooth.
2. Adjust seasoning as desired.

How to Use:

Serve as a topping for vegetables, meats, rice, or beans.

Precautions:

Use in moderation if prone to cilantro sensitivity or allergic to coriander.

Golden Turmeric Rice

Function: Anti-inflammatory and supports liver and joint health.

Ingredients:

- 1 cup basmati rice
- 2 cups water or broth
- 1 tsp turmeric powder
- 1/2 tsp black pepper
- 1 tbsp ghee or olive oil
- Salt to taste

Instructions:

1. Sauté turmeric in ghee or oil for 1 minute.
2. Add rice, stir to coat, then add liquid and bring to boil.
3. Simmer covered 18–20 minutes until cooked.

How to Use:

Serve as a vibrant side dish or base for meals.

Precautions:

Turmeric may interact with blood thinners; consult a physician if on medication.

Basil & Oregano Tomato Sauce

Function: Antioxidant-rich and supports immune function.

Ingredients:

- 2 cups fresh tomatoes (or 1 can crushed)
- 1 tbsp olive oil
- 2 garlic cloves
- 1 tsp dried oregano
- 1 tbsp chopped fresh basil
- Salt and pepper to taste

Instructions:

1. Sauté garlic in olive oil.
2. Add tomatoes, oregano, and simmer for 20 minutes.
3. Stir in fresh basil just before serving.

How to Use:

Serve over pasta, grains, or vegetables.

Precautions:

None for general use, though tomatoes may cause acid issues in sensitive individuals.

Oatstraw Vanilla Latte

Function: Strengthens nervous system and remineralizes the body.

Ingredients:

- 2 tbsp dried oatstraw
- 1.5 cups water
- 1/2 cup milk or milk alternative
- 1/2 tsp vanilla extract
- 1 tsp honey (optional)

Instructions:

1. Simmer oatstraw in water for 20 minutes.
2. Strain and combine with warm milk, vanilla, and sweetener.
3. Whisk or froth and serve warm.

How to Use:

Enjoy in the morning or afternoon to promote calm focus.

Precautions:

Oatstraw is generally safe but check for cross-contamination if gluten-sensitive.

Garlic & Rosemary Infused Oil

Function: Antimicrobial and anti-inflammatory; supports immune and heart health.

Ingredients:

- 1 cup olive oil
- 3 garlic cloves, sliced
- 1 tbsp dried rosemary

Instructions:

1. Gently heat olive oil with garlic and rosemary on low for 15–20 minutes.
2. Do not let it smoke.
3. Cool, strain, and store in a clean glass jar.

How to Use:

Use for sautéing vegetables, drizzling over dishes, or as a bread dip.

Precautions:

- Refrigerate and use within 1–2 weeks to avoid risk of botulism from garlic oil.
- Avoid if sensitive to garlic or rosemary.

Parsley-Lemon Green Sprinkle

Function: Rich in chlorophyll and vitamin C; supports detox and immunity.

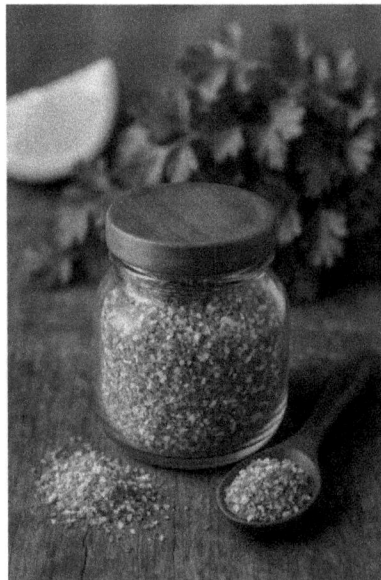

Ingredients:

- 1/4 cup dried parsley
- 1 tbsp lemon zest (dried)
- 1 tsp sea salt

Instructions:

1. Blend all ingredients in a spice grinder or by hand.
2. Store in a spice shaker or glass jar.

How to Use:

Sprinkle on salads, eggs, roasted veggies, or grains.

Precautions:

High doses of parsley may stimulate the uterus — avoid large amounts during pregnancy.

Marshmallow Root Breakfast Porridge

Function: Soothes gut lining, supports digestion, and relieves irritation.

Ingredients:

- 1/2 cup rolled oats
- 1 tsp marshmallow root powder
- 1.5 cups water or milk
- 1/2 tsp cinnamon
- 1 tsp honey (optional)

Instructions:

1. Combine all ingredients in a small pot.
2. Simmer for 8–10 minutes, stirring often.
3. Serve warm.

How to Use:

Eat in the morning to coat and soothe the gut.

Precautions:

May delay absorption of medications — take herbs or prescriptions at different times.

Dill & Chive Yogurt Sauce

Function: Supports digestion and freshens breath.

Ingredients:

- 1 cup plain yogurt
- 1 tbsp fresh dill (or 1 tsp dried)
- 1 tbsp chopped fresh chives
- 1/2 tsp lemon juice
- Salt to taste

Instructions:

1. Stir all ingredients together in a bowl.
2. Chill for 30 minutes before serving for best flavor.

How to Use:

Use as dip for vegetables or topping for baked potatoes and fish.

Precautions:

Dairy-based — use a plant yogurt if lactose intolerant.

Peppermint-Cocoa Herbal Bark

Function: Uplifts mood and soothes digestion; a delightful herbal treat.

Ingredients:

- 1 cup dark chocolate chips
- 1 tsp dried peppermint (crushed)
- 1 tbsp cocoa nibs (optional)
- Pinch of sea salt

Instructions:

1. Melt chocolate chips in a double boiler or microwave.
2. Stir in peppermint and cocoa nibs.
3. Spread onto parchment-lined tray and sprinkle with sea salt.
4. Chill until firm, then break into pieces.

How to Use:

Enjoy 1–2 pieces after meals or as a mood-lifting snack.

Precautions:

Contains caffeine from cocoa and may interfere with sleep if eaten late.

Lemon Verbena Honey Drizzle

Function: Brightens mood, calms nerves, and enhances digestion.

Ingredients:

- 1/4 cup dried lemon verbena
- 1 cup raw honey

Instructions:

1. Place lemon verbena in a clean glass jar.
2. Warm honey until just pourable (not hot).
3. Pour over the herbs to cover and stir to remove air bubbles.
4. Let infuse for 5–7 days, then strain.

How to Use:

Drizzle over yogurt, toast, tea, or fruit.

Precautions:

- Avoid heating the honey too much to preserve enzymes.
- Not for infants under 1 year.

Cinnamon Hawthorn Berry Syrup

Function: Supports heart health and improves circulation.

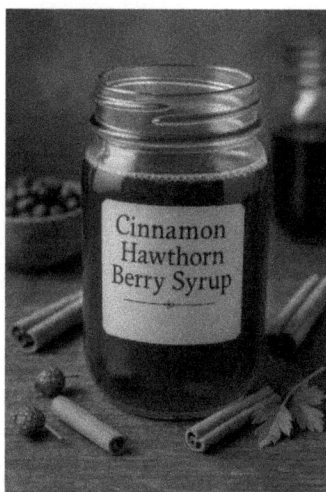

Ingredients:

- 1/2 cup dried hawthorn berries
- 1 cinnamon stick
- 3 cups water
- 1 cup honey

Instructions:

1. Simmer hawthorn and cinnamon in water for 30–40 minutes.
2. Strain and reduce to about 1.5 cups of liquid.
3. Add honey while warm and stir until dissolved.
4. Store in the fridge up to 1 month.

How to Use:

Take 1–2 teaspoons daily or mix into warm water or tea.

Precautions:

Consult with a doctor if on blood pressure or heart medications.

Bitter Greens Herb Salad Mix

Function: Stimulates digestion and bile flow.

Ingredients:

- 1/2 cup chopped dandelion greens
- 1/4 cup chopped arugula
- 2 tbsp chopped fresh parsley
- 1 tbsp fresh mint
- Olive oil and lemon juice (to dress)

Instructions:

1. Mix all greens and herbs in a large bowl.
2. Drizzle with olive oil and lemon juice just before serving.

How to Use

Eat before meals as a digestive appetizer.

Precautions

Bitter herbs may aggravate ulcers or gallbladder issues if used in excess.

Elderberry Vinaigrette

Function: Immune-boosting and antioxidant-rich.

Ingredients:

- 2 tbsp elderberry syrup
- 1/4 cup apple cider vinegar
- 1/4 cup olive oil
- 1 tsp Dijon mustard
- Pinch of salt

Instructions:

1. Whisk all ingredients together in a small bowl or jar.
2. Shake well before each use.

How to Use:

Use on leafy salads or drizzle over steamed vegetables.

Precautions:

Use cooked or prepared elderberries only; raw berries can be toxic.

Holy Basil (Tulsi) Rice Bowl

Function: Balances blood sugar, supports mood and resilience to stress.

Ingredients:
- 1 cup cooked brown rice
- 1/4 cup chopped fresh tulsi leaves (or 1 tbsp dried)
- 1 tbsp olive oil
- 1 garlic clove, minced
- Salt and sesame seeds to garnish

Instructions:

1. Heat oil in a pan, sauté garlic and tulsi for 2–3 minutes.
2. Stir into cooked rice and season with salt.
3. Top with sesame seeds if desired.

How to Use:

Eat as a nourishing lunch or stress-relieving dinner base.

Precautions:

Holy basil may lower blood sugar; monitor if diabetic or on insulin.

Stinging Nettle Pesto

Function: Rich in minerals; supports energy and iron levels.

Ingredients:

- 2 cups fresh nettle leaves (blanched)
- 1/2 cup olive oil
- 1/4 cup walnuts or sunflower seeds

- 2 garlic cloves
- 1/4 cup grated hard cheese (optional)
- Salt and lemon juice to taste

Instructions:

1. Blanch nettles in boiling water for 1–2 minutes, then drain and cool.
2. Combine all ingredients in a food processor.
3. Blend until smooth, adding more oil if needed.
4. Adjust seasoning to taste.

How to Use:

Toss with pasta, spread on toast, or serve as a dip.

Precautions:

- Use gloves when handling raw nettles to avoid stings.
- Ensure they are well-cooked before eating.

Thyme & Lemon Immune Broth

Function: Clears respiratory pathways and enhances immune function.

Ingredients:

- 1 onion, chopped
- 2 garlic cloves, smashed
- 1 tbsp fresh thyme (or 1 tsp dried)
- Juice of 1 lemon
- 4 cups vegetable broth
- 1 tbsp olive oil
- Salt and pepper to taste

Instructions:

1. Sauté onion and garlic in olive oil until translucent.
2. Add broth and thyme, simmer for 15 minutes.
3. Stir in lemon juice and season to taste.
4. Strain if desired for a clear broth.

How to Use:

Drink as a warm tonic or use as a base for soups.

Precautions:

Avoid thyme in large medicinal doses during pregnancy.

Rosemary Apple Cider Reduction

Function: Supports digestion, improves circulation, and adds flavor depth.

Ingredients:

- 1 cup apple cider vinegar
- 1 tbsp dried rosemary
- 1 tsp honey (optional)

Instructions:

1. Simmer vinegar and rosemary gently for 10–15 minutes.
2. Strain and stir in honey while warm.
3. Cool and store in a glass jar.

How to Use:

Use as a glaze for roasted vegetables or meats.

Precautions:

Highly acidic — avoid use on sensitive teeth or open mouth sores.

Basil & Lemon Balm Salad Dressing

Function: Uplifting and calming; supports digestion and mood.

Ingredients:

- 1/4 cup olive oil
- 1 tbsp apple cider vinegar
- 1 tsp dried lemon balm
- 1 tsp dried basil
- 1/2 tsp Dijon mustard
- Salt and pepper to taste

Instructions:

1. Whisk all ingredients together until emulsified.
2. Let sit 10 minutes before serving to blend flavors.

How to Use:

Drizzle over fresh greens or grain salads.

Precautions:

Lemon balm may interfere with thyroid medication; consult if needed.

Reishi Mushroom Cacao Elixir

Function: Supports immunity, reduces stress, and provides gentle stimulation.

Ingredients:

- 1 cup milk or plant milk
- 1 tsp reishi mushroom powder
- 1 tbsp raw cacao powder
- 1 tsp maple syrup or honey
- 1/4 tsp cinnamon

Instructions:

1. Gently heat all ingredients in a saucepan until warm.
2. Whisk or blend for a frothy consistency.
3. Do not boil.

How to Use:

Drink in the morning or afternoon for an energizing, immune-tonic treat.

Precautions:

Reishi may lower blood pressure; consult your doctor if on antihypertensives.

Chapter 12

Seasonal Wellness Planning

By now, you've learned to blend tinctures, stir salves, and stir herbs into nourishing broths and comforting cups of tea. You've started weaving herbs into your kitchen and medicine cabinet—but there's another layer to herbal living that deepens the experience: *seasonal alignment*.

Nature isn't static. Neither are we. Just as the seasons change—bringing shifts in light, temperature, and energy—our bodies and needs transform too. Herbalism, at its core, is about **living in rhythm** with these natural cycles. This chapter helps you plan your wellness practices in harmony with the seasons, using herbs that gently support your body's changing needs throughout the year.

Spring: Awaken, Cleanse & Rebuild

Seasonal Energy:

Spring marks a fresh start. After the inward stillness of winter, the body is ready to stretch, awaken, and release the stagnation of the cold months. Energy begins to rise, metabolism quickens, and organs like the liver, kidneys, and lymphatic system become more active.

Spring Herbal Goals:

- Stimulate liver & lymphatic detox
- Replenish mineral stores
- Clear out digestive sluggishness
- Gently support mood transitions

Key Herbs:

- *Dandelion Root & Leaf* – promotes liver function and gentle diuresis
- *Nettle* – rich in iron, calcium, and trace minerals for rebuilding
- *Cleavers* – supports lymph drainage and puffiness reduction
- *Burdock Root* – skin-purifying and blood-strengthening
- *Lemon Balm* – uplifts and calms springtime restlessness

Daily Practices:

- Begin mornings with a **nettle and lemon balm infusion** for mineral restoration.
- Add **dandelion leaves** to fresh salads or blend into green smoothies.
- Try a **cleavers tincture or tea** as a gentle lymphatic cleanser for 2–3 weeks.
- Stir burdock into broths or grain bowls as a cooling root vegetable.

"Spring is not about extremes. It's about gentle nudges—like opening the windows and letting in new air."

Summer: Cool, Calm & Protect

Seasonal Energy:

With longer days and stronger sun, summer brings vibrant outward energy. But with that brightness also comes heat, inflammation, travel stress, and potential overexertion. The body now benefits from herbs that **cool**, **hydrate**, and **nourish nerves and skin**.

Summer Herbal Goals:

- Regulate body temperature
- Hydrate tissues
- Calm heat-triggered irritability
- Support digestion in the heat

Key Herbs:

- *Hibiscus* – rich in antioxidants, lowers internal heat
- *Peppermint & Spearmint* – cooling and digestive
- *Chamomile* – soothes tension, helps with sun-disrupted sleep
- *Rose Petals* – emotional coolant and heart opener
- *Elderflower* – supports sinus and respiratory clarity

Daily Practices:

- Keep a pitcher of **hibiscus and mint sun tea** in your fridge all summer.
- Add **rose petal-infused honey** to yogurt or fruit for an elegant finish.
- Use **elderflower tincture** to support seasonal allergies or combine with lemon in spritzers.
- Sip **chilled chamomile tea** during hot afternoons or post-beach rest.

"Summer is vibrant but volatile. Herbs help us stay cool—not just in temperature, but in temperament."

Fall: Ground, Fortify & Prepare

Seasonal Energy:

Fall is the bridge between summer's outward energy and winter's deep retreat. Our focus shifts to preparing our bodies for the colder months ahead: **building immunity**, **supporting digestion**, and **anchoring routines**.

Fall Herbal Goals:

- Strengthen immune function
- Support digestion and gut flora
- Begin warming the system
- Calm stress and nervous system

Key Herbs:

- *Astragalus* – a foundational immune tonic for long-term use
- *Ginger Root* – stimulates digestion and warms the core
- *Echinacea* – fast-acting at first sign of sickness
- *Thyme & Sage* – antimicrobial, protect throat and lungs
- *Schisandra* – adaptogenic and stress-balancing

Daily Practices:

- Start simmering **astragalus and ginger decoctions** to sip during chilly evenings.
- Infuse **thyme and sage honey** as a throat protector before school or work.
- Incorporate **echinacea** only when symptoms begin—not daily.
- Use **warming digestive spices** like cinnamon, cardamom, and clove in food and tea.

"Fall is for stacking wood, preserving food, and bolstering the body's foundation before the frost."

Winter: Rest, Rebuild & Restore

Seasonal Energy:

Winter is the most yin season—quiet, introspective, slow. It's a time for **deep nourishment**, **nervous system rest**, and immune fortification. Herbs now work like warm blankets and woodstoves—providing insulation, strength, and calm.

227

Winter Herbal Goals:

- Restore adrenal and nervous system balance
- Deepen sleep and mental rest
- Warm digestion and circulation
- Strengthen respiratory and immune defenses

Key Herbs:

- *Reishi & Chaga* – mushroom allies for immunity and resilience
- *Ashwagandha* – supports sleep, mood, and stress recovery
- *Licorice Root* – gentle adrenal tonic and respiratory soother
- *Cinnamon, Ginger, Clove* – circulatory and warming
- *Oatstraw* – rich in silica and B vitamins for nerves and vitality

Daily Practices:

- Brew a **reishi and cinnamon mushroom chai** with milk and honey.
- Add **ashwagandha powder** to warm almond milk before bed.
- Incorporate **warming digestive teas** after meals (like ginger and fennel).
- Simmer **adaptogen broths** with roots and mushrooms weekly.

"Winter is not the absence of life—it's the deepening of it. Let your herbal practices go inward with you."

Closing Reflection…

Seasonal herbalism is not another item on your to-do list. It's a way of *living with the Earth*, of tending your body with the same care you might tend a garden. Whether you drink tulsi in spring or stir mushrooms into winter broth, you're honoring the cycles that sustain all life.

You don't need to be perfect. Start small. Maybe it's a seasonal tea, a kitchen herb added with intention, or a moment of stillness that aligns you with what the season is asking of you.

Let this chapter guide your way—not only through the calendar—but deeper into a life lived in rhythm.

Final Thoughts: Coming Home to Herbalism

As you reach the final pages of this book, pause—breathe—and feel the transformation that has taken root within you.

You began this journey with curiosity. Maybe you were seeking gentle healing. Perhaps a deeper connection to nature. Or maybe you felt a calling—one passed down through the stories of your grandmothers, the pull of the wild plants underfoot, or the ache for more sovereignty over your health.

Whatever brought you here, you now hold something precious: **a living, breathing relationship with the herbal world.**

Throughout these pages, you've learned more than recipes and remedies. You've stepped into an age-old lineage. You've studied not only plants, but rhythm, intuition, and balance. Let's revisit how far you've come:

In the Beginning...

You explored the *foundations of herbalism*, discovering the history, ethics, and philosophies that remind us herbs are not just tools—but allies, teachers, and kin.

You learned to identify, harvest, and honor the **Top 40 Must-Have Herbs**—trusting the dandelions, chamomile, tulsi, and nettle that now grow at the edge of your kitchen, your path, and your life.

In the Apothecary...

You mastered the art of **tinctures, extracts, salves, and balms**—realizing that medicine can be made with your own hands, with time, intention, and love.
You created healing from simplicity: a mason jar, a root, a spoon, a whisper of prayer.

In the Kitchen...

You learned that **medicine and nourishment are one and the same**. From broths that restore minerals to ghee that soothes the gut, you now know how to infuse your meals with life-giving plants.

Your meals have become rituals. Your teas, moments of mindfulness. Your spices, tiny apothecaries in a bowl.

In Daily Living...

You discovered that herbalism isn't just something you do—it's a way of being.

You've tuned into the seasons:

☀ Cooling in summer
🍂 Grounding in fall
❄ Rebuilding in winter
🌱 Cleansing in spring

You've come to understand that health is not about perfection—it's about *partnership* with your body and with nature.

And Now...

You no longer need to look outside yourself for every answer. You know how to listen.

You've learned to trust the subtle wisdom of a tea that calms you. The quiet intuition that says, "Add ginger today. Rest more tonight. Brew a tea for grief."

This is what herbalism is at its core—not quick fixes or pills or trends.

It is a remembering.
It is a return.
It is coming home.

Final Words...

Let this be your compass as you move forward:

- Start small. One herb. One tea. One act of care. That's enough.
- Trust your senses. Smell, taste, listen. They are ancient tools.
- Learn from the land where you live. Local herbs know your climate, your people, your story.
- Don't be afraid to make mistakes. Herbalism is forgiving, just like the plants.
- Keep learning. This book is your seed, but the roots grow with practice, with patience, and with love.

And finally...

Share what you've learned. Herbal wisdom multiplies when shared. Teach your children, your neighbors, your friends. Plant herbs in your garden, in community spaces, in windowsills. Let this knowledge ripple outward like chamomile seeds in the wind.

Because when you heal with herbs, you're not just healing yourself—you're healing the world.

Thank you for walking this path.
The plants are waiting. Your apothecary is ready.
And your journey has only just begun.

With green blessings,
❧ *The Herbal Path is Yours Now.*